Chuck Poole

The Path to Depth
Charles E. Poole

© 2022
Published in the United States by Nurturing Faith Inc., Macon Ga.,
Nurturing Faith is a book imprint of Good Faith Media (www.goodfaithmedia.org).

Library of Congress Cataloging-in-Publication Data is available.

ISBN: # 978-1-63528-196-5
All rights reserved. Printed in the United States of America.

All scripture citations are taken from the New Revised Standard Version (NRSV) unless otherwise indicated.

Cover Photo:
"High Above the Clouds in Glacier National Park." Copyright Bruce Gourley.
Visit brucegourley.com for information.

To Marcia
Josh and Bett
Ansley, Emma Kate, Charlotte, Walker, and Ailey
Maria and James
Mary Hazel, Marcia, David, Mason, and Brock

Contents

vi
Preface

viii
Acknowledgments

Part One: The Narrow Way

2
Swimming Inward, Floating Outward

5
Another Day

9
All Conversions Are Approximate

13
Concerning Prayer

17
Through Suffering

21
At the Intersection of Light and Pain

25
On Not Being Offended by Jesus

28
Concerning Justice and Righteousness

32
Heart Writing

36
Further

Part Two: The Wide Place

40
Anchors and Sails

44
Nine Words

50
Dear Miss Marietta

55
Todos Somos Inmigrantes

59
The Hour Is Coming, and Is Now Here

63
Faith Beyond the Boundaries

67
But What About John 14:6?

72
On Not Being Sad About What God Is Glad About

78
Fields and Forests, Seas and Trees

82
The Journey Jonah Never Took

85
Epilogue

86
Notes

Preface

"The path to depth" is a simple name for the never-ending journey to a deeper life with God. A phrase that first appears in my daily prayer journals on May 6, 2007, the path to depth came to me on a small trail in a thick forest near High Falls, Georgia, when I noticed how the path I was walking kept disappearing, then reappearing, at every turn and bend; a narrow, winding way that, it occurred to me, was not unlike the path to a deeper life with God—the path to depth.

"The path to depth" sounds a little like "the path to death." Which, in a way, it is:

…a path to death that is also a path to life; as in "We are crucified with Christ, nevertheless, we live."

…dying to an old way of life, as Paul said in his letter to the Romans, to rise and walk in a new way of life—a deeper, wider life with God;

…what scripture sometimes calls "walking in the Spirit" or "growing in grace";

…the life the late Mary Oliver captured so beautifully with her single simple sentence, "Another morning, and I wake, with thirst, for the goodness I do not have."[1]

For many seekers of every faith, myself among them, that is the story of our lifelong journey: thirsting for the goodness we do not yet have; longing for a deeper life with God, not because we think we must be better so we can persuade God to love us, and not because we think that the better we do in this life the more rewarded we will be in the next life.

Rather, we wake each morning with the desire to live more deeply, fully, and faithfully because, as far as we know, this is the only life we are ever going to have in this world. While no one can say for certain, as far as we know, we are not going to get to come back around, do this over, and get it right the next time. So we long to get on, and stay on, the path to depth so that we can live the one and only life we are ever going to have as deeply, fully, and faithfully as we can.

The path to depth is a narrow way; narrow, not as in exclusive, but as in centering; a lifelong reaching for a more thoughtful, mindful, centered life; praying, each day, all through the day, to be kind and gentle, brave and true.

However, while the path to depth is a narrow way, it leads to a wide place. On the path to depth, the deeper we go, the wider we grow. The longer we stay on the narrow way, the wider we draw our circle of welcome, hospitality, friendship, and grace, until, eventually, the size of the circumference of the circle of our welcome is the same as the size of the circumference of the circle of welcome around God.

I, myself, am still a seeker on the path to depth, with a far way yet to go, and much failing and growing yet to do. Which is to say that these "sermons for seekers" are not offered from a sure-footed guide on the path to depth as much as from a fellow traveler, stumbling forward, seeking a way of knowing God and loving the world that will lead, at last, to the wide place of boundless grace that awaits us all at the far end of the narrow way: the path to depth.

— Charles E. Poole
Pentecost, 2022

The way down and the way up are the same.
—Heraclitus

Acknowledgments

Tom Long, in his very helpful book, *What Shall We Say?* resurrects that beautiful old Latin phrase, *solvitur ambulando*, which means "solved by walking."[2] Which, in my experience, has almost always been the case: new light on old truth coming to us slowly, eventually, while walking in the Spirit of God with the people of God—*solvitur ambulando*.

For all the people of God alongside whom I have been blessed to walk, I offer, in this space, my deepest gratitude:

- the dear and good souls at Log Cabin Baptist Church in Macon, Georgia, who formed my mother, my father, my sister, and me in ways as well as they knew;

- all the friends in each of the congregations since, who, across the years, have surrounded and supported Marcia, Joshua, Maria, and me;

- writers, thinkers, poets, and teachers I have not met in person, but who, nonetheless, have stretched my mind and spirit, leading me to places I might never have gone alone—Fred Buechner, Barbara Brown Taylor, Mary Oliver, Martin Luther King Jr., Naomi Shihab Nye, Richard Rohr, and Marilynne Robinson, to name a few—for all of whom I am deeply grateful.

Among the many guides who have helped me find my way along the path to depth, I would like to thank, in this space:

- Kirby Godsey and Walter Shurden, who have embodied the Spirit of God for me in ways that have left me forever in their debt;

- the Northminster family of faith, a congregation of dear and good souls who have gently drawn the trajectory of my life toward an arc of love and truth I might never have known without them.

To all of these, who have been walking partners on the path to depth—*solvitur ambulando* friends and teachers, mentors and guides—I offer my deepest gratitude; with special thanksgiving to, and for, Marcia, and the beloved family that has grown around us, to whom this small work is dedicated, with much love.

"Lake McDonald Twin Reflections Black and White," copyright Bruce Gourley.

Part One
The Narrow Way

Swimming Inward, Floating Outward

Present your bodies as a living sacrifice, holy and acceptable to God, which is your spiritual worship. Do not be conformed to this world, but be transformed by the renewing of your minds, so that you may discern what is the will of God—what is good and acceptable and perfect.

For by the grace given to me I say to everyone among you not to think of yourself more highly than you ought to think, but to think with sober judgment, each according to the measure of faith that God has assigned. For as in one body we have many members, and not all the members have the same function, so we, who are many, are one body in Christ, and individually we are members one of another. We have gifts that differ according to the grace given to us: prophecy, in proportion to faith; ministry, in ministering; the teacher, in teaching; the exhorter, in exhortation; the giver, in generosity; the leader, in diligence; the compassionate, in cheerfulness.

Romans 12:1-8

"I appeal to you therefore, by the mercies of God, to present your bodies as a living sacrifice, holy and acceptable to God, which is your spiritual worship. Do not be conformed to this world, but be transformed by the renewing of your minds." With those words, this reading from Romans brings us to the place where the path to depth begins; those many moments in life when we open our minds to be changed by God and offer our lives to be used by God.

Paul's call for us to be transformed by the renewing of our minds is clearly an invitation to change. Those words, "be transformed by the renewing of your minds," call us to a life of openness; thinking, praying, pondering, asking, seeking, waiting; following the new light the Holy Spirit gives us until we are transformed, truly changed.

That life of openness to the Spirit is part of what it means to get on, and stay on, the path to a deeper life with God—opening our minds to be changed by God. And, another part of life on the path to depth is offering our lives to be used by God.

The path to a deeper life with God is not only about exploring, with our minds, the truth of God; it is also about incarnating, in our bodies, the love of God. Or, as Paul said in our scripture, "presenting our bodies as living sacrifices"—embodying the love and care of God in the world.

The Path to Depth

More than fifty years ago a group of women, all then in their thirties and forties, went to the fair grounds on High Street in Jackson, Mississippi, to take sandwiches to the Freedom Riders who had been arrested in Jackson and were being held there. One of them, now in her nineties, told me, "We went because we just knew it was the right thing to do." To borrow Paul's phrase, they were "presenting their bodies as living sacrifices holy and acceptable to God."

Which, Paul says, is our "spiritual worship." "Present your bodies as living sacrifices to God," Paul writes, "which is your spiritual worship." All those small, simple, physical things we do that embody the love and care of God are, according to Paul, acts of spiritual worship.

Which is the way life looks on the path to a deeper life with God; the lines that once separated the physical part of our lives from the spiritual part blend, blur, and fade. The spiritual becomes physical, and the physical becomes spiritual, as we present our bodies as living sacrifices.

We get on the path to depth by opening our minds to be changed by God and by offering our lives to be used by God. And then, we spend the rest of our lives walking that same path—our minds ever open to see whatever new light the Holy Spirit gives, our bodies ever open to do the smallest acts of physical kindness.

This is the life that Mary Oliver once described as "swimming inward" and "floating outward."[3] We get up every morning and do the daily work of swimming inward; praying, each day, all through the day, to be more mindful with our words, more gentle with our judgments, more liberal in our embrace, more kind and brave, more brave and kind, until all that intentional swimming inward eventually causes us to start instinctively floating outward.

The same things we once thought impossible to do, we now find impossible not to do. Now, we are so transformed that we can't not sit down with and stand up for the same people Jesus would sit down with and stand up for—those who are marginalized, ostracized, demonized, dehumanized, oppressed, vulnerable, left out, and alone. Now, we can't not embody the love of God wherever life is hardest and worst: all that going deeper in our life with God causing us to grow wider in our love for the world; all that prayerful swimming inward eventually becoming a life of floating outward.

So this is how you swim inward,
So this is how you float outward,
So this is how you pray.
—**Mary Oliver**

Another Day

Finally, be strong in the Lord and in the strength of his power. Put on the whole armor of God, so that you may be able to stand against the wiles of the devil. For our struggle is not against enemies of blood and flesh, but against the rulers, against the authorities, against the cosmic powers of this present darkness, against the spiritual forces of evil in the heavenly places. Therefore take up the whole armor of God, so that you may be able to withstand on that evil day, and having done everything, to stand firm. Stand therefore, and fasten the belt of truth around your waist, and put on the breastplate of righteousness. As shoes for your feet put on whatever will make you ready to proclaim the gospel of peace. With all of these, take the shield of faith, with which you will be able to quench all the flaming arrows of the evil one. Take the helmet of salvation, and the sword of the Spirit, which is the word of God.

Pray in the Spirit at all times in every prayer and supplication. To that end keep alert and always persevere in supplication for all the saints. Pray also for me, so that when I speak, a message may be given to me to make known with boldness the mystery of the gospel, for which I am an ambassador in chains. Pray that I may declare it boldly, as I must speak.

Ephesians 6:10-20

"Put on the whole armor of God." Whenever we encounter those words from the one who wrote the letter to the Ephesians, it is important for us to remember that putting on the whole armor of God is not something we do all at once, or once and for all, but, rather, over and over, day after day, getting up every morning and preparing ourselves to face another day.

To put on the whole armor of God is to get ready, to prepare ourselves to face whatever is coming next, to center ourselves spiritually, so that we might actually go through an entire day in a thoughtful, mindful, prayerful way; ready to live deeply, fully, and faithfully into each new moment and conversation; paying attention to, and seeing the image of God in, every person who crosses our path that day.

Which is why putting on the whole armor of God is something we have to do all over again, with each new day. Some people do this by reading from scripture each morning; some by going on a long, slow prayer walk, or a morning run; others by sitting silently for a few moments in centering prayer. Some turn to a favorite podcast, or daily devotional guide, such as Henri Nowen's *Bread for the Journey*, Richard Rohr's *Yes, And,* or Mary Oliver's *Devotion*. Others find writing in a daily prayer journal to be a helpful centering discipline.

Some do all of the above. And, some do little of the above, not because they don't want to, but because, from morning to night, their household is an incessant blur of family responsibility that leaves little space for any stillness of any kind.

In her book, *Eat, Pray, Love,* Elizabeth Gilbert tells about renting a small cabin on the isolated island of Gili Meno, and embarking there on a silent retreat, a spiritual retreat Gilbert launched with the vow that she was closing her mouth, and would not open it until something inside her had changed—the kind of retreat many of us might love to take, but a stillness few of us can afford.[4] Rather, most of us have to put on the whole armor of God, a little here and a little there, when and where and how we can.

But, for even the most hurried and breathless of us, some kind of daily centering of the soul is important, because that is how we get ready to face whatever we might face, that day, in a mindful, thoughtful, prayerful way.

All of which is to say that what this passage calls putting on the whole armor of God is a spiritual discipline as daily as waking up and getting up, to start, all over again, another day; the dailyness Mary Oliver captured with that simple, beautiful prayer, "Another morning, and I wake, with thirst, for the goodness I do not have."[5]

Which is a truly beautiful, deeply spiritual way to live,

…waking each morning with thirst for the goodness we do not yet have;

…our daily longing to take another step along the path to depth;

…like the days of creation in the book of Genesis, each new day building on, but going beyond, the day before;

…each new day bent with the weight of every day already done, but free from the weight of every day yet to come;

…each new day, another day to practice living in a mindful, thoughtful, prayerful way;

…putting on the whole armor of God;

…staying ready every day to live deeply, fully, and faithfully into, and through, whatever is coming next, by getting ready each day to live deeply, fully, and faithfully into, and through, whatever is coming next.

*Today is the day to which all your yesterdays have been
leading since the hour of your birth.
It is the point from which all your tomorrows will proceed
until the hour of your death.
If you were aware of how precious today is,
you could hardly live through it.
Unless you are aware of how precious it is,
you can hardly be said to be living at all.*
—**Fred Buechner**

All Conversions Are Approximate

I do not understand my own actions. For I do not do what I want, but I do the very thing I hate. Now if I do what I do not want, I agree that the law is good. But in fact it is no longer I that do it, but sin that dwells within me. For I know that nothing good dwells within me, that is, in my flesh. I can will what is right, but I cannot do it. For I do not do the good I want, but the evil I do not want is what I do. Now if I do what I do not want, it is no longer I that do it, but sin that dwells within me.

So I find it to be a law that when I want to do what is good, evil lies close at hand. For I delight in the law of God in my inmost self, but I see in my members another law at war with the law of my mind, making me captive to the law of sin that dwells in my members. Wretched man that I am! Who will rescue me from this body of death? Thanks be to God through Jesus Christ our Lord!

So then, with my mind I am a slave to the law of God, but with my flesh I am a slave to the law of sin.

Romans 7:15-25

"I do not understand my own actions … I do not do the good I want, but the wrong I do not want is what I do." Students of scripture have often wondered whether those words describe Paul's life before or after his baptism, some saying that it seems unlikely, at the time of the writing of Romans, Paul would still be struggling to do the right thing so long after his conversion and baptism.

But what Paul describes here sounds, to me, like the life of every baptized person I have ever known: each of us, broken in some way; all of us, perpetually longing for a deeper goodness we do not yet have, reaching, day after day, for a deeper life with God.

We keep striving for that deeper goodness we do not yet have, not because we think we must do better for God in order to be loved better by God, and not because we think a more centered, thoughtful, prayerful life will gain us a reward, or spare us a punishment. Rather, we, with Paul, long to live mindful, thoughtful, centered lives of goodness, kindness, and righteousness because, as far as we know, this is the only life we are ever going to have, and we want to live it as deeply, fully, and faithfully as we can.

If we knew we were going to get to come back around, do this over and get it right next time, perhaps it wouldn't matter so much how we live this life. But, while no one can say for certain, as far as we know, this life is the one and only life we are ever going to have in this world. Which is why we keep striving for a deeper life with God, because we don't want to spend the one and only life we are ever going to have being reckless and careless, hard and graceless, glib and shallow, deceptive and manipulative, sarcastic and unkind.

No one wants to spend their one and only life that way. What we want is what Paul wanted: to get on, and stay on, the path to a deeper life with God—a more thoughtful, prayerful, mindful, gentle life of courage, kindness, spiritual depth, and careful, truthful speech.

But, like Paul, our deep desire for genuine righteousness notwithstanding, we often fail. Like Paul, we want to live lives of unfailing goodness and truth, but we often end up doing what we don't want to do, after which comes the inevitable self-loathing and self-doubt, until, in our frustration with our own selves we say, with Paul, "O wretched soul that I am, who will deliver me from this complex, complicated, contradiction of a life I am living?"

One answer to that holy discontentment might be found in Evelyn Underhill's memorable sentence, "We must reach for what we do not have by the faithful practice of what we do have." We reach for the unfailingly thoughtful, mindful, prayerful life we do not have by the faithful practice of our desire to be that way.

And, the more we practice being thoughtful, mindful, prayerful, truthful, gentle, generous, agendaless and kind, the better we get at it until, eventually, we begin to become more that way than once we were. It doesn't happen all at once, or once and for all. But, little by little, step by step, we can actually go farther along the path to depth; reaching for the unfailing goodness we do not have by the faithful practice of the spiritual longing we do have.

All of which calls to mind, for me, an article I once read about a minister in an Episcopal church in London who, before entering the ministry, had served as an auctioneer at Sotheby's. Near the end of the article, the reporter who was interviewing the auctioneer-turned-pastor asked if he had noticed any similarities between the auction house and the church, to which the minister replied: "Actually, there is one way in which they are the same. Back in the pre-computer days when I worked at Sotheby's, we would write, each day, on a big chalkboard the currency exchange rates—British pounds to American dollars, and other conversion rates relevant to our customers. However, since those currency conversion rates would sometimes change during the day, we would always write, across the bottom of the board, **ALL CONVERSIONS ARE APPROXIMATE.** Which I have found to be true, as well, in the church."[6]

Indeed, all conversions are approximate, never complete, or perfect—a lifelong journey on the path to depth, reaching for the mindful, thoughtful life we do not have by the faithful practice of the desire for a mindful, thoughtful life we do have; always longing for, and reaching for, a deeper life with God.

*I am so distant from the hope of myself,
in which I have goodness, and discernment,
and never hurry through the world
but walk slowly, and bow often.*
—Mary Oliver

Concerning Prayer

Likewise the Spirit helps us in our weakness; for we do not know how to pray as we ought, but that very Spirit intercedes with sighs too deep for words. And God, who searches the heart, knows what is the mind of the Spirit, because the Spirit intercedes for the saints according to the will of God.

We know that all things work together for good for those who love God, who are called according to God's purpose.

Romans 8:26-28

"We do not know how to pray as we ought to pray." With those words, Paul helps us embrace the truth that there is much we do not know about prayer. But then, Paul says we should go ahead and pray anyway, because the Holy Spirit will take the prayers we do not know how to pray or say, and give them to God in sighs too deep for words.

This way of looking at prayer can be a great relief to those who grew up, as did I, with the kind of theology that sees prayer as a transaction; a view of prayer that raises many familiar questions about "how prayer works," questions such as:

- If I have enough faith, can I get God to give me what I need?

- If I pray hard enough, often enough, long enough, can I persuade God to do my will?

- If I get enough prayer partners to join me in praying for what I need, will God be moved to do what God would not have done if only one voice asked instead of one thousand?

Like countless others, I grew up asking those kinds of questions, thinking of prayer as something I had to get right, as though prayer was a transaction between myself and God, which would fail or prevail, based on how many hours of prayer, or partners in prayer, I gave God.

But then, across many years, as I watched people of equal faith pray with equal persistence for equally important blessings, I noticed that some received the gift and some didn't. And it didn't matter if they were in a conservative church or a liberal church, Pentecostal or liturgical, Christians, Muslims, Sikhs, Hindus, or Jews: prayers moved mountains about as often in one place as they did in the other. Having watched all that for many years, I finally came to see that there is no formula or recipe for "successful" praying. Rather, for reasons no one can explain, sometimes prayer changes our circumstances, and sometimes our circumstances change our prayers.

Sometimes, we pray for healing or deliverance or reconciliation, and, thanks be to God, we receive it. Those are the times when prayer changes our circumstances. And, sometimes, we pray for healing or deliverance or reconciliation, and we don't receive it. Those are the times when our circumstances change our prayers.

When that happens, we don't stop praying or give up on God. Rather, we adjust our prayers to the trajectory of our lives, praying for the next best thing. We start out praying for all to be well and the biopsy results to be clear. If they aren't, we pray for the treatment to be successful. If it isn't, we pray for comfortable days and restful nights—our prayers chasing our lives, from the best hope to the next hope to the last hope.

Or, we start out praying for the conflict to be miraculously resolved. If it isn't, we pray for the healing work of reconciliation. If that doesn't happen, we then pray for comfort and courage for all who must grieve forward the future pain of the broken relationship—our prayers chasing our lives, from the best hope to the next hope to the last hope.

A lifetime spent stumbling prayerfully along the path to a deeper life with God keeps teaching us that sometimes prayer changes our circumstances, and sometimes our circumstances change our prayers. But, either way, still we pray:

…telling God the truth about what we hope and fear and want and need, and trusting God to help us live deeply, fully, and faithfully the life that is ours to live;

…"praying without ceasing," not because we should, but because we can't not;

…living even the most ordinary of days in such a mindful, thoughtful, prayerful way that, as someone once said of a chance encounter with Martin Luther King Jr., "I couldn't tell if Dr. King was talking with me or praying for me," our conversations eventually becoming as gentle and healing, quiet and true as our prayers—one, indiscernible from the other.

Such is the life of prayer on the path to depth... The path to depth is the life of prayer, and the life of prayer is the path to depth.

*I know a lot of fancy words.
I tear them from my mouth,
And then I pray.*
—Mary Oliver

Through Suffering

And the Lord restored the fortunes of Job when he had prayed for his friends; and the Lord gave Job twice as much as he had before. Then there came to him all his brothers and sisters and all who had known him before, and they ate bread with him in his house; they showed him sympathy and comforted him for all the evil that the Lord had brought upon him; and each of them gave him a piece of money and a gold ring. The Lord blessed the latter days of Job more than his beginning; and he had fourteen thousand sheep, six thousand camels, a thousand yoke of oxen, and a thousand donkeys. He also had seven sons and three daughters. He named the first Jemimah, the second Keziah, and the third Keren-happuch. In all the land there were no women so beautiful as Job's daughters; and their father gave them an inheritance along with their brothers. After this Job lived one hundred and forty years, and saw his children, and his children's children, four generations. And Job died, old and full of days.

Job 42:10-17

"And the Lord restored the fortunes of Job, and gave Job twice as much as Job had before." Those words, from the end of the book of Job, never fail to call to mind, for me, that beautiful old saying attributed to Beverly Gaventa: "Things will not always hurt the way they do now."

Which, perhaps, was the case for Job. Once Job made it as far as chapter 42, perhaps things did not hurt as deeply as they did back in chapters 1 and 2, when so much pain and loss broke Job's heart and crushed Job's spirit.

Perhaps, but who can say for sure? After all, the children Job loved and lost, back at the beginning of the book of Job, would never, for Job, be less lost or less loved. So, who can say how much of Job's pain had settled and eased by the time Job emerged, from his long struggle, with what Job 42 calls "twice as much" … a happy ending to a sad story, but a happy ending with which we must take great care, lest we lapse into a "sunny side of the street" expectation that the ending to every sorrow will be as neat and tidy as the last chapter of Job's story.

Which is not to say that sorrow never leads to something good. To the contrary, sorrow and loss often lead us to a more thoughtful, mindful, kind, and gentle life than ever we might have known without our sorrow or trouble, tragedy or loss; a truth that leads some to say that

God sends us trouble to make us better and that God allows tragedy to break our hearts so we can emerge from the darkness more gentle and kind—all suffering, a part of the plan of God.

This is a popular way of thinking, and, while I do not share it, I understand why so many are drawn to it as a way of making sense of life. I, myself, once embraced this way of thinking. But, then, it occurred to me that to continue to say that *all* suffering was either sent to us or allowed for us, in the will and plan of God, would require me to assign even the most violent and evil things to the will and plan of God, and, for me, that was to sacrifice too much of the goodness and love of God on the altar of the sovereignty and control of God.

However, while I do not believe that everything which happens is always in God's plan, I do believe that all of us are always in God's hands and that God is always at work in our lives, in joy and in sorrow, to bring us into a deeper, more thoughtful, mindful, kind, and gentle way of being in the world; pain and struggle opening us up to God and others in ways that often leave us, like Job, with "twice as much"—not twice as much security or power, comfort or success, but twice as much empathy and understanding, kindness and compassion—the path to depth, more often than not, going though suffering.

Rarely has anyone captured that possibility more beautifully than Naomi Shihab Nye in her poem, "Kindness," in which she writes, "Before you can learn the tender gravity of kindness, before you can know kindness as the deepest thing inside, you must first know sorrow as the other deepest thing. You must wake up with sorrow. You must speak to it until your voice catches the thread of all sorrows, and you see the size of sorrow's cloth. Then," she continues, "It is only kindness that makes sense anymore, only kindness that ties your shoes and sends you out into the day … going with you everywhere like a shadow or a friend."[7]

Pain and sadness can do that in us, and for us. Because pain is as surgical as surgery is painful, pain and sorrow, struggle and loss can, indeed, open us up that deeply—the path to depth, winding its steep, quiet way through suffering.

It isn't guaranteed, of course. We don't always emerge from sorrow twice as thoughtful and gentle, empathetic and kind. But we can. And,

The Path to Depth

more often than not, we do. Somehow, the Spirit of God finds a new opening in our brokenness.

…pain, as Barbara Brown Taylor once observed, "Burning away everything extra, everything trivial, everything petty and less than noble, until we become see-through with light…"[8]

…our own version of Job's twice-as-much, our arms twice as open, our words twice as gentle, our spirit twice as patient, welcoming, empathetic, and kind as we were before the sorrow and the pain…

…emerging from our worst and hardest struggles with what Howard Thurman called the "quiet eyes"[9] of those who have suffered, and what Mary Oliver called "the resolute kindness of those who have eaten the dark hours…"[10]

…twice as kind than ever we would have been without the pain, not because God planned or sent our greatest sorrows, but because the God who holds and carries, with us and for us, our greatest sorrows, is the God who wrings whatever good can be wrung from the hardest and worst that life can do; the God who raised Jesus from the grave, bringing whatever is left from whatever was lost, until that far-off someday when finally, eternally, things will no longer hurt the way they do now…

This Me

I was on my way to becoming
The one I was going to be.
But then something happened
And so much changed
That, instead, I became this me.

We all start out with an empty page,
Our horizons as wide as the sea.
But when what happens, happens,
Life narrows down,
Until all we can be is this me.

When what happens, happens,
All we can be
Is the most kind and gentle
Truthful and tender, me we can be.
—CEP

At the Intersection of Light and Pain

I know a person in Christ who fourteen years ago was caught up to the third heaven—whether in the body or out of the body I do not know; God knows. And I know that such a person—whether in the body or out of the body I do not know; God knows— was caught up into Paradise and heard things that are not to be told, that no mortal is permitted to repeat. On behalf of such a one I will boast, but on my own behalf I will not boast, except of my weaknesses. But if I wish to boast, I will not be a fool, for I will be speaking the truth. But I refrain from it, so that no one may think better of me than what is seen in me or heard from me, even considering the exceptional character of the revelations. Therefore, to keep me from being too elated, a thorn was given me in the flesh, a messenger of Satan to torment me, to keep me from being too elated. Three times I appealed to the Lord about this, that it would leave me, but he said to me, "My grace is sufficient for you, for power is made perfect in weakness." So, I will boast all the more gladly of my weaknesses, so that the power of Christ may dwell in me. Therefore I am content with weaknesses, insults, hardships, persecutions, and calamities for the sake of Christ; for whenever I am weak, then I am strong.

2 Corinthians 12:2-10

Paul's testimony that God was strongest where Paul was weakest calls to mind Ernest Hemingway's remarkable sentence, "The world breaks everyone, and, afterward, many are strong at the broken places."[11]

Which is so often the case, not for all who suffer and struggle, but, certainly, for many.

Think, for example, of Frederick Buechner, his life forever changed by the sadness of his father's suicide, but, a sadness from which Buechner has given so many so much light by which to live.

Or, think of Anne Lamott, who, through her own battles with brokenness, has given so many weary souls so many words of grace.

And think of Henri Nowen, who, from the depth of his own self-doubt, has given the rest of us so much light for the journey.

And, of course, there's Mother Teresa, whose unparalleled empathy rose, in part, from a pain so deep that she is reported once to have said, "If I make it into heaven, and they let me say only one sentence to Jesus, I know what it will be: 'All my life, I loved you in the darkness.'"

... Fred Buechner, Anne Lamott, Henri Nowen, Mother Teresa: all, like Paul, strong at the broken places, some of their greatest light rising from some of their deepest pain. Which is sometimes true for many of us, as well: our strongest kindness shaped by our hardest struggles; our most gentle empathy rising from our most difficult grief; our deepest pain, the source of our deepest insights.

And, sometimes, also, the other way around: While it is often true that our deepest pain can lead to some of our deepest insights, it is also sometimes true that our deepest insights can lead to some of our deepest pain.

When I was a seminary student, for example, in my mid-twenties, discovering the truth that the Bible, inspired and inspiring, beautiful and wonderful as it is, was never intended to be God's inerrant, infallible, literal, last word plunged me into an uncertainty so deep I can still only describe it as "emotional paralysis," not because what I had discovered wasn't true, but, to the contrary: because it was so obviously true, but so very different from what I had always thought, and been taught.

As the years went on, and a life of prayerful walking in the Holy Spirit revealed to me more and more spiritual light and new insight, there would be more and more spiritual growing pains, as I discovered truths that, to many, are basic and fundamental, but that, to me, were altogether new:

...revelations such as the truth that God calls people to ministry without regard for whether they happen to be male or female;

...the truth that same-sex life and love is a human difference, not a spiritual sin;

...the truth that the God who created the universe thirteen billion years ago cannot be completely captured in any one religion, including my own;

...each new revelation helpful and true, but each one becoming, for me, what Paul's revelations were for him: not only another source, at last, of light, but also another source, at first, of pain.

The poet W.H. Auden once said, "We would rather die in our dread than climb the cross of the moment and let our illusions die,"[12] which is something I understand. I understand why people would sometimes rather go to their grave with less truth than go through their life with more truth, because following new light on old truth and letting our long-held assumptions die can make the path to depth a painful place—not unlike what happened to Paul.

For Paul, a painful new thorn in the flesh was the price of admission to whatever those revelations were that Paul said he saw on his journey to paradise. The same is so for all of us; new light bringing pain as surely as pain brings new light, none of the pain sent to us from God, but all of the pain used for us by God to help us become deeper and stronger, more gentle, thoughtful, courageous, kind, and true.

Pain makes theologians of us all.
　—**Barbara Brown Taylor**

On Not Being Offended by Jesus

When John heard in prison what the Messiah was doing, he sent word by his disciples and said to him, "Are you the one who is to come, or are we to wait for another?" Jesus answered them, "Go and tell John what you hear and see: the blind receive their sight, the lame walk, the lepers are cleansed, the deaf hear, the dead are raised, and the poor have good news brought to them. And blessed is anyone who takes no offense at me."

As they went away, Jesus began to speak to the crowds about John: "What did you go out into the wilderness to look at? A reed shaken by the wind? What then did you go out to see? Someone dressed in soft robes? Look, those who wear soft robes are in royal palaces. What then did you go out to see? A prophet? Yes, I tell you, and more than a prophet. This is the one about whom it is written, 'See, I am sending my messenger ahead of you, who will prepare your way before you.' Truly I tell you, among those born of women no one has arisen greater than John the Baptist; yet the least in the kingdom of heaven is greater than he.

Matthew 11:2-11

It appears that John the Baptist does not know exactly what to think about Jesus; sending messengers to ask Jesus, "Are you the one we have been waiting for, or should we look for another?" To which Jesus replies, "Go tell John that the blind see, the deaf hear, the lame walk, lepers are cleansed, the dead are raised, and the poor receive good news. And blessed is anyone who is not offended at me"—an answer for John, which is also a reminder for us, that Jesus can only be who Jesus is.

Jesus cannot become who John the Baptist, or we, might want or wish Jesus to be. Jesus can only do what he does and be who he is. Read the four gospels, and what you see is the only Jesus Jesus can be, the Jesus whose moral compass is as true as his wingspan is wide.

…Jesus' moral compass getting him *in* trouble;

…Jesus' wingspan drawing him *to* trouble—what the late Congressman John Lewis called "good trouble, necessary trouble":

…Jesus' moral compass causing him to stand up against injustice;

…Jesus' wingspan causing him to stand up for the marginalized and the oppressed, the hurting and the poor.

And blessed is anyone who takes no offense at Jesus for saying what he says, doing what he does, and being who he is. Jesus is always going to sit down with and stand up for whoever is in the toughest spot and the hardest place, and blessed is anyone who takes no offense at Jesus for always ending up *on* the side of, and *at* the side of, whoever is most marginalized, ostracized, demonized, dehumanized, stigmatized, vulnerable, oppressed, left out, outcast, and alone. Jesus' straight-up moral compass of justice and all-out wingspan of welcome will not let Jesus do anything else.

Which is why the longer any person travels the path to depth, and the closer any person gets to Jesus, the more predictable they become. Every time any issue comes up, you don't have to wonder where they will be, because they will always be where Jesus would be. They don't stand up against oppression and injustice in all its forms because they have made a political decision to be progressive; they stand up against oppression and injustice in all its forms because they have made a spiritual decision to be Christian—

…Christian, as in not offended by Jesus;

…Christian, as in so filled with the spirit of Jesus that they become predictable in their response to every issue that arises, always ending up on the same side of every question: the side where Jesus would be if Jesus were here;

…not the conventional wisdom, traditional values, Jesus of popular Bible Belt Christianity;

…not the I-20 Jesus who dominates the religious landscape from Atlanta to Dallas;

…not that Jesus, but the real Jesus, the Jesus at whom we get our best look in the four gospels.

And blessed is anyone who takes no offense at that Jesus, and no offense at those who long to live with a moral compass of social justice and a wingspan of joyful welcome as straight-up and all-out as the moral compass and wingspan of Jesus.

Bible Belt Jesus

We thought we had the answers,
Settled, clear and sure;
Who was in and who was out,
What was wrong and who was pure.

But Jesus won't wear our Bible belt,
Buckled snug and tight,
All the answers written down,
To be read in black and white.

We like to think he thinks like us,
And we've got all the light.
But Jesus won't wear our Bible belt,
Buckled up that tight.
—CEP

Concerning Justice and Righteousness

Alas for you who desire the day of the Lord! Why do you want the day of the Lord? It is darkness, not light; as if someone fled from a lion, and was met by a bear; or went into the house and rested a hand against the wall, and was bitten by a snake. Is not the day of the Lord darkness, not light, and gloom with no bright ness in it?

I hate, I despise your festivals, and I take no delight in your solemn assemblies. Even though you offer me your burnt offerings and grain offerings, I will not accept them; and the offerings of well-being of your fat ted animals I will not look upon. Take away from me the noise of your songs; I will not listen to the melody of your harps. But let justice roll down like waters, and righteousness like an ever-flowing stream.

Amos 5:18-24

"Let justice roll down like waters, and righteousness like an ever-flowing stream." Those words from the book of Amos belong to a long line of Bible verses in which the words "justice" and "righteousness" hold hands, including:

- Genesis 18:19, which says the way of the Lord is justice and righteousness;
- Psalm 33:5, which says God loves justice and righteousness;
- Psalm 99:4, which says God acts with justice and righteousness;
- Proverbs 21:3, which says God cares more about justice and righteousness than sacrifices and offerings;
- Jeremiah 22:3, which says God calls us to live lives of justice and righteousness.

Those two words, justice and righteousness, which appear together so frequently in our English language Bibles, sometimes come from the same Hebrew root, a word that means "to make things right," which can actually make it difficult to differentiate justice from righteousness. My best effort at distinguishing one from the other is, admittedly, sort of "cornbread and peas" in its simplicity, but it goes like this:

The Path to Depth

- righteousness, the inside part of our life with God; justice, the outside part of our life with God
- righteousness, the inner life of truth and integrity; justice, the outer life of kindness and compassion
- righteousness, the True North moral compass of our soul; justice, the stretched-out wingspan of our spirit
- righteousness, our deeper life with God; justice, our wider life with others—the public work of justice growing, most often, from the inner work of righteousness

As our longing to live a righteous life keeps drawing us into a deeper life with God, that ever-deeper devotion to righteousness results in an ever-wider commitment to fairness and equality, hospitality and welcome, inclusion and justice for all persons.

To read, again, all four gospels—Mathew, Mark, Luke, and John—is to see, again, the truth that the closer we get to the Jesus of the four gospels, the more serious we become about justice for whoever is most marginalized, ostracized, stigmatized, demonized, and dehumanized. When we truly have Jesus in our heart, standing up for the same people Jesus would stand up for by standing up against the same things Jesus would stand up against becomes one of those things we can't not do.

As Peter Storey says, when we ask Jesus to come into our heart, Jesus always answers, "Only if I can bring my friends."[13] And, if you have ever read the four gospels, you know that when Jesus brings Jesus' friends into our hearts, Jesus brings the last first: whoever is most outcast, vulnerable, shunned, slighted, lonely, left out, and alone—all coming in with Jesus. Otherwise, Jesus won't come, because, if the four gospels are a trustworthy record of the words and works of Jesus, Jesus' life was all about that public, visible, clear, courageous kind of righteousness the Bible calls justice.

That kind of life, the kind that begins in righteousness and ends in justice, is the kind of life I call "conservative in the mirror and liberal through the window." When we look at ourselves in the mirror, we hold ourselves to the most rigorous demands of righteousness, and when we look at others through the window, we embrace the world in a welcome of justice that is as liberal as the boundless embrace of God.

Watch the greatest souls you know: They all have their flaws, limits, blind spots, and failures, of course. But, the more conservative they become about Jesus, the more liberal they become about issues of social justice and human equality—a life of expansive piety; *piety*, because it is a life grounded in righteousness; *expansive*, because it is a life stretched by justice.

What a way to live: walking prayerfully along the path to depth until we go so deep with God and grow so close to Jesus that, in our ordinary, everyday lives, justice *does* roll down like waters, and righteousness like an ever-flowing stream; our longing for righteousness taking us ever deeper into God and our passion for justice taking us ever wider into the world.

The arc of the moral universe is long, but it bends toward justice.
　　　　—Martin Luther King Jr.

Heart Writing

The days are surely coming, says the Lord, when I will make a new covenant with the house of Israel and the house of Judah. It will not be like the covenant that I made with their ancestors when I took them by the hand to bring them out of the land of Egypt—a covenant that they broke, though I was their husband, says the Lord. But this is the covenant that I will make with the house of Israel after those days, says the Lord: I will put my law within them, and I will write it on their hearts; and I will be their God, and they shall be my people. No longer shall they teach one another, or say to each other, "Know the Lord," for they shall all know me, from the least of them to the greatest, says the Lord; for I will forgive their iniquity, and remember their sin no more.

Jeremiah 31:31-34

"The days are surely coming, says the Lord, when I will make a new covenant with my people. It will not be like the covenant that I made with their ancestors, says the Lord. This time, I will write it on their hearts." To read those words from the book of Jeremiah is to know, instinctively, that we are in the presence of one of the Bible's great tipping points: the moment when God is reported to have said, to Jeremiah, "The days are surely coming when I am going to make a new covenant with my people. But, this time, I am going to write it on their hearts."

The days of which God spoke were not only surely coming, but also already arriving. By the time Jeremiah told the people of God that God was going to write a new covenant on their hearts, the heart writing Jeremiah was promising was already happening.

For example, back in the book of Deuteronomy, both eunuchs and foreign-born persons were excluded from the covenant of God with the people of God, but in Isaiah 56, the writer says, "Of course immigrants and eunuchs are welcome in the family of God." In fact, in Jeremiah 38, it is a foreign-born eunuch who is the hero: an Ethiopian eunuch named Ebedmelech, rescuing Jeremiah from a pit into which Jeremiah had been thrown to die. And, in the same part of the Hebrew scripture that first says "no" to the eunuchs to whom Isaiah and Jeremiah eventually say "yes," Moabites are also specifically, and permanently, excluded from ever being a part of the family of God. But the book of Ruth not only makes a Moabite the hero of the story, but it also weaves her into the family tree of David, making a previously permanently excluded Moabite the grandmother of Israel's greatest king.

Something is happening. Lines are being redrawn, not between Judaism and Christianity, Old Testament and New, but even as Jeremiah speaks. Even as Jeremiah is dreaming of a day when God will rewrite God's law on human hearts, God is already doing it—the children of God, following their hearts past the place where the letter of the law once would have dropped them off.

…A new law of love that begins in the Old Testament, and continues in the New, nowhere more clearly than in that moment in the gospel of John when Jesus follows his heart past the place where his Bible would have dropped him off, in the face of a crowd with rocks at the ready to stone a person found in adultery; that moment at which John 8 reports that when the crowd reminded Jesus that it was written in scripture that the person should die, Jesus bent down, not once, but twice, to write, and then rewrite, something in the sand.

John does not let us see what Jesus writes in the sand. Which means, of course, that, since no one knows what Jesus wrote, then rewrote, we all get to wonder. I wonder if Jesus may have been writing in the sand a new law of love that will, from time to time, like all words written in sand, need to be rewritten—the lines we draw in the sand, needing to be redrawn from time to time, to meet the growing demands of a living law of love written, not on paper pages, but on pounding hearts:

…something to which Jesus points when Jesus says, in Matthew 22:34-40, that the central standard by which all the law is to be measured is the commandment to love God with all that is in us, and to love all others as we love ourselves;

…not unlike Paul's declaration in Romans 13 that all the laws and commandments can be summed up in one: "Love others as you love yourself";

…Second Testament echoes of Jeremiah's First Testament promise: "The day is coming when God will lay down a new law for the people of God. And, this time, God is going to write it on human hearts."

The church has a name for that kind of heart writing. We call it the Holy Spirit. When we open our lives to the Spirit of God, what God wants for us and from us moves, more and more, into our hearts until eventually we become so completely born again and so deeply filled with the Spirit of God that we no longer need any external law or rule, chapter or verse, incentive or motivation, reward or punishment. All we need is what we have: the law of love, written on our hearts.

In fact, if we live prayerfully enough for long enough, intentionally open to the Holy Spirit, we may actually reach a place in our lives at which if, for some reason, someone were to come around and take up all the Bibles—while that would be to us an enormous loss—it would not change the way we live or what we do or how we treat others, because the Holy Spirit has already written what matters most all over the walls of our hearts—the walls of our hearts covered in the graffiti of God; the law of love, just as Jeremiah promised, written on our hearts.

*The Bible is its own kind of miracle,
but I hope never to put the book
ahead of the people the book calls me to love.*
—Barbara Brown Taylor

Further

I still have many things to say to you, but you cannot bear them now. When the Spirit of truth comes, he will guide you into all the truth; for he will not speak on his own, but will speak whatever he hears, and he will declare to you the things that are to come. He will glorify me, because he will take what is mine and declare it to you. All that the Father has is mine. For this reason I said that he will take what is mine and declare it to you.

John 16:12-15

"I still have many things to say to you, but you cannot bear them now. When the Spirit of truth comes, the Spirit will guide you into all the truth." Those words from John's gospel are, for many of us, the story of our life: the Holy Spirit taking us further and further into truth that, at one time in our life, we could not bear;

…slowly, slowly, little by little, across a lifetime of praying and thinking, thinking and praying, the Holy Spirit taking us further and further along the path of spiritual depth, until, eventually, the same truth we once could not bear to hear, we now cannot bear to hide;

…the same truth we once feared so greatly, we could not bear to hear it, we now believe so deeply, we cannot bear to hide it;

…our experience, a living, breathing echo of what Jesus described to his first friends in this gospel lesson, where Jesus is reported to have said: "I still have many things to say to you, but you cannot bear them now. When the Spirit of truth comes, the Spirit will guide you into all the truth."

But, of course, that raises the question, "How do we discern whether or not what we are seeing and hearing is the leadership of the Holy Spirit?"—a question to which the answer waits in the next verses of this gospel passage, where Jesus is reported to have said, "The Spirit will not speak on the Spirit's own, but will take what is mine and declare it to you." I cannot speak for you, but, as for me, that is the measure of whether or not a nudge or whisper is from the Holy Spirit: "Is it true to the spirit of Jesus? Is what I believe the Holy Spirit is leading me to say or do true to the spirit of Jesus?" (Not the Jesus of popular Bible Belt Christianity, but the Jesus of the four gospels; the Jesus who said that what matters most is that we love God with all that is in us, and that we love all others as we want all others to love us.)

The Holy Spirit will always only take us further along that same path, the path down which Jesus got us started; the path of truth and love, justice and mercy, courage and kindness down which Jesus got us started, before he handed us off to the Holy Spirit to take us the rest of the way; further and further along the narrow way of truth that leads, at last, to a wide place of grace.

Has Truth been advancing among you?
—An old Quaker question

Part Two
The Wide Place

Anchors and Sails

Jesus, full of the Holy Spirit, returned from the Jordan and was led by the Spirit in the wilder ness, where for forty days he was tempted by the devil. He ate nothing at all during those days, and when they were over, he was famished. The devil said to him, "If you are the Son of God, command this stone to become a loaf of bread." Jesus answered him, "It is written, 'One does not live by bread alone.'"

Then the devil led him up and showed him in an instant all the kingdoms of the world. And the devil said to him, "To you I will give their glory and all this authority; for it has been given over to me, and I give it to anyone I please. If you, then, will worship me, it will all be yours." Jesus answered him, "It is written, 'Worship the Lord your God, and serve only him.'"

Then the devil took him to Jerusalem, and placed him on the pinnacle of the temple, saying to him, "If you are the Son of God, throw yourself down from here, for it is written, 'He will command his angels concerning you, to protect you,' and 'On their hands they will bear you up, so that you will not dash your foot against a stone.'" Jesus answered him, "It is said, 'Do not put the Lord your God to the test.'" When the devil had finished every test, he departed from him until an opportune time.

Luke 4:1-13

"Then the devil took Jesus to Jerusalem, and placed him on the pinnacle of the temple, saying to him, 'If you are the Son of God, throw yourself down from here, for it is written, "God will command the angels to protect you, and on their hands they will bear you up, so that you will not dash your foot against a stone."' And Jesus answered the devil, 'It is written, "Do not put the Lord your God to the test."'"

Every three years the lectionary asks the church throughout the world to read those words on the First Sunday in Lent. And, every time they roll back around, we get to watch while Jesus and the devil face off in a contest of these verses versus those verses, with the devil quoting Psalm 91:11-12 ("God will command the angels to protect you, so that you will not dash your foot against a stone") and Jesus quoting Deuteronomy 6:16 ("Do not put the Lord your God to the test")— the devil, actually using a verse of scripture to tempt Jesus to do God's work the world's way; quoting the Bible accurately, but using the Bible wrongly. Which, needless to say, wasn't the last time a Bible verse was quoted accurately, but used wrongly. In the world of my origins, for example:

- We quoted 1 Corinthians 14:35 accurately, but used it wrongly to exclude women from ministry.
- We quoted Mark 10:11-12 accurately, but used it wrongly to penalize those who had suffered through the sorrow of divorce.
- We quoted Leviticus 18:22 accurately, but used it wrongly to condemn same-sex life and love, sending the Bible on errands the Bible wasn't written to run.

We quoted the Bible accurately, but used the Bible wrongly; a way of handling scripture that created second-class citizens in the family of faith; a sin for which we can be forgiven, but from which it is too late to undo the harm done to dear and good people by folk like myself, who used the Bible literally on others (1 Cor. 14:35, Mark 10:11-12, Lev. 18:22) in ways we would never apply the Bible literally to ourselves (Matt. 5:39, Luke 14:33, 1 Tim. 2:9); taking a stand on the verses that worked for us, and taking a pass on the verses that didn't.

The remedy for which is to decide to be content to use our Bible only the way Jesus used his. If I belonged to another faith, I'm sure I would have a different measure for how to interpret scripture. But, because I am a Christian, my measure for the interpretation of scripture is Jesus. This is why I keep saying, when it comes to how we handle our Bible, the most important passage in the Bible is Matthew 22:34-40, because this is the passage where Jesus says all the law and the prophets are to be interpreted in the light of love for God and love for others. "All the law and prophets" is all the Bible Jesus had. So, when Jesus said that all the law and the prophets are to be read in the light of love for God and love for others, that tells us how Jesus handled his Bible.

In John 8, for example, Jesus reached past the place where Deuteronomy 22:22 might have told him to stop, and sent the one who was caught in adultery home to begin her life again. And, in Mark 3, Jesus reached past the place where Exodus 20:10 might have dropped him off, and healed the man with the withered hand without requiring him to wait until the Sabbath had passed. Jesus was clearly not living his life by a scripture here and a scripture there, but, rather, as Mary Oliver once wonderfully said, "in accordance with a single certainty."[14] And, for Jesus, that single certainty by which he read all scripture and saw all people appears to have been the single certainty that nothing matters more than loving God with all that is in us and loving others the way we want others to love us.

There are many things Jesus did that we cannot do, but we can handle our Bible the way Jesus handled his; reading the whole Bible in the light of love for God and love for others, even when that means going past the place where a Bible verse might have dropped us off.

I think of it as lowering an anchor and raising a sail. We lower our anchor into the Bible by reading and studying the Bible, saying and hearing the Bible's words until they become the muscle-memory of our soul; dropping our anchor deep into the waves of the Bible while, simultaneously, keeping our sail always up for the wind of the Spirit: because we know that, when the Bible was canonized in the fourth century, the Holy Spirit did not go into retirement.

When the Bible was finally finished and settled on by the church at the end of that long process called "canonization," the Holy Spirit did not buy a condo in Destin and retire. Rather, the Holy Spirit continues to nudge, tug, reveal, and speak—which means that the wind of the Spirit can still send us sailing, beckoning us further and further along the path to depth ... sometimes, even, past the place where a verse of scripture might have dropped us off.

> When Christians pretend that every line in the Bible
> is of equal importance and inspiration,
> they are being very unlike Jesus.
> —Richard Rohr

Nine Words

When the Pharisees heard that he had silenced the Sadducees, they gathered together, and one of them asked Jesus a question to test him. "Teacher, which commandment in the law is the greatest?" Jesus said to him, "'You shall love the Lord your God with all your heart, and with all your soul, and with all your mind.' This is the greatest and first commandment. And a second is like it: 'You shall love your neighbor as yourself.' On these two commandments hang all the law and the prophets."

Matthew 22:34-40

Samesexuality is a human difference, not a spiritual sin. Because of the religious world in which my life was first formed, it has taken me a lifetime on the path to a deeper life with God to learn to say that single, simple sentence—nine words that, at the risk of sounding naïve and simplistic, I believe hold the answer to the religious world's long struggle concerning same-sex life and love.

There isn't any spiritual difference between gay people of God and straight people of God. We all worship, sing, pray, serve, try, and fail the same. Whether we are straight or gay, we all have the same capacity to be moral or immoral, kind or mean, careful or reckless, righteous or unjust, generous or selfish.

Across the centuries, too much of the church has too often failed to embrace the truth that persons who are gay are just as likely as persons who are not gay to be prayerful people of integrity and goodness, called by God to lead and serve in the name and spirit of Jesus. As a result, too much of the church has too often, for too long, made it difficult for gay persons to claim, not only their full human identity, but, also their full spiritual identity as prayerful, spirit-filled children of God—as though you can't be a serious Christian and be a gay, lesbian, bisexual, or transgender person. That relegation of persons to the edges of the church is a fear-driven marginalization for which we should repent and beyond which we should move, because, until love finally drives out fear, fear will continue to drive out love.

All of this finally came clear to me roughly two decades ago while sitting by the bed of a dying man in a nursing home, a man who had lived a long life of integrity and fidelity, prayer and devotion, who happened to be gay. As I sat near his bed in the last weeks of his life, it occurred to me that he and I were different from one another only in that I was a straight person—a human difference, not a spiritual one.

Of course, given our long history of turning to scripture to support what we believe, that raises the important question: "But what about what the Bible says concerning same-sex life and love?"[15]

The Bible includes several passages that are often assumed to address same-sex life and love. There appear to be seven such passages. (I say "appear to be" because it is not clear how many of them actually address a committed relationship between two adults of the same sex.)

Take, for example, the first of those seven passages: the story of the city of Sodom in Genesis 19. Often pointed to as a story about God's judgment against same-sex life and love, Genesis 19:1-11 recalls the story of men who attempted to sexually assault Lot's angelic visitors; an attempt at sexual violence that everyone on the planet condemns, but that has nothing to do with a relationship between two people of the same sex.

In the Old Testament, there are two more passages that are often invoked to condemn same-sex relationships: "You shall not lie with a male as with a woman; it is an abomination" (Lev. 18:22) and "If a man lies with a male as with a woman, both of them have committed an abomination, they shall be put to death (Lev. 20:13)." Those words belong to a Levitical "holiness code" that also prohibits the eating of pork (Lev. 11:7-12), forbids rough beards (Lev. 19:27), and excludes from worship leadership anyone with blemished skin, failing eyesight, or poor posture (Lev. 21:16-20)—verses to which no Christians I know assign any continuing authority.

That leaves the four New Testament passages about same-sex relationships. One is Jude 1:7, which refers to the aforementioned passage in Genesis 19. Two more are 1 Corinthians 6:9-10 and 1 Timothy 1:10, both of which are on the list of possible passages because they contain the word "sodomite," which could be a reference to what we think of as a same-sex relationship, but which also may refer to the sexual exploitation of boys by men—something everyone condemns, but something that has no more relation to a same-sex relationship between two adults than the heterosexual exploitation of children has to sexual intimacy between a man and a woman.[16]

Of the seven Bible passages often assumed to be about same-sex intimacy, those are six, which leaves one: Romans 1:25-31, which says:

> Because they exchanged the truth about God for a lie, and worshiped and served the creature rather than the Creator ... God gave them up to degrading passions. Their women exchanged natural intercourse for unnatural, and in the same way also the men, giving up natural intercourse with women, were consumed with passion for one another.... And since they did not see fit to acknowledge God, God gave them up to a debased mind and to things that should not be done.

Because of the part of this passage that refers to "a way of intercourse which is not natural," this passage is sometimes assumed to be Paul's indictment of same-sex life and love, which it may be. But, to read the full paragraph is to see that it also describes those of whom Paul speaks as being "God haters" who are full of envy, murder, and malice, which does not describe any of the gay persons I have known, who are no more or less likely to be God-haters who are full of envy, murder, and malice than any of the straight people I have known. Whoever Paul is describing in Romans 1, he is not describing the prayerful, thoughtful child of God who happens to be a gay person and for whom same-sex life and love *is* their "natural inclination."

All of which is to say that, of the seven passages in the Bible that are often assumed to be about same-sex intimacy, it isn't clear which ones, if any, address committed same-sex relationships.

But, even if some of those seven passages do apply to same-sex relationships, most of the Christians I know would not be able to say that it was because of their commitment to the authority of the Bible that they held a religious objection against gay and lesbian persons, because most of the Christians I know continue to own possessions, resist evildoers, and wear jewelry—in spite of what the Bible says in Luke 14:33, Matthew 5:39, and 1 Timothy 2:9. This is not to say that there is something wrong with owning possessions, resisting evildoers, or wearing jewelry, but it is to say that there is something wrong with using the Bible on others in ways we would never apply the Bible to ourselves.

The Path to Depth

I believe that our world's popular religious judgments about gay, lesbian, bisexual, and transgender persons have less to do with the Bible than with the way we were raised—what we've always thought and been taught. One very large factor, especially for many men who grew up, as did I, in the Deep South Bible Belt of the twentieth century is that much of our thinking about persons who are gay was shaped more by immature masculinity than by mature Christianity. At school, at work, and even in the church, we emphasized our masculinity by ridiculing those who were drawn to persons of their same sex. (The sin, in that case, was not the sexuality of those who are gay, but the meanness of those who are straight.)

In the religious world of my origins, we talked a lot about Jesus. But when it came to how we treated those who were beyond the boundaries of our comfortable majority, we often failed to embody the spirit of Jesus. Which is one reason why people in our part of the world who had a gay or lesbian son or daughter often encouraged them to move to New York or San Francisco, where they might be more safe from hurt and harm than in the Bible Belt. Ponder, for a moment, this tragic irony: The part of the country that claims the most followers of Jesus is one of the most difficult parts of the country in which to be who one is, a sad commentary on how far the popular Christianity of the Bible Belt has strayed from the Jesus of the four gospels.

As far as we know, that Jesus, the Jesus of the four gospels, never said anything about same-sex relationships. He did, however, have something to say about what matters most in life. When asked in Matthew 22 what matters most, Jesus is reported to have said that what matters most is that we love God with all that is in us, and that we love our neighbors as we love ourselves—reading all scripture, and seeing all persons, in the light of, and through the lens of, love. Which is not unlike what we find in Matthew 7:12, where Jesus is reported to have summed up all the law and the prophets in a single simple sentence of nine simple words: Treat others as you would have others treat you—one small example of which I heard described in an interview shortly after the death of President George Herbert Walker Bush.

In early December of 2018, as the world mourned the death of President Bush, National Public Radio (NPR) aired a conversation in which two women, Bonnie Clement and Helen Thorgalson, who own a store near the Bush's home in Kennebunkport, Maine, remembered with much affection and gratitude the gladness and warmth with which their longtime friend, George H.W. Bush, had served, with all joy and no hesitation, as a witness at their wedding; a small example from President Bush concerning how to relate to gay and lesbian loved ones and friends: as loved ones and friends, without making one part of their life, their sexual orientation, the most interesting or important part of their life, seeing that human difference for what it is—a human difference, not a spiritual sin.

To learn to discern the difference between a difference and a sin is an important step along the path to spiritual depth, which, for me, has meant coming to see, and say, the truth that travels in those nine simple words: Samesexuality is a human difference, not a spiritual sin:

…truth that many sincere people of faith do not embrace, but truth that many others have always instinctively known;

…truth that many more may someday come to see, and say, *not in spite of* the fact that they are prayerful, Spirit-filled, serious Christians, *but because of* the fact that they are prayerful, Spirit-filled, serious Christians.

Not until the sun refuses you do I refuse you.
—Walt Whitman

Dear Miss Marietta

In everything do to others as you would have them do to you; for this is the law and the prophets.

Matthew 7:12

On April 3, 1968, Martin Luther King Jr. preached his famous "I have been to the mountaintop" sermon to an enthusiastic congregation, on a stormy evening, in Memphis, Tennessee. The next day, he died. All these years later, I don't remember where I was or what I was doing when I heard that Dr. King had been assassinated. I do, however, remember feeling a compelling need to find Marietta Green, a person of color, who was my friend and the custodian at the church my family attended, Log Cabin Baptist Church on Napier Avenue in Macon, Georgia.

So, as soon as I could slip away, I rode my bike to the church, found "Miss Marietta," and said to her, "I heard about Mr. King being killed. I wanted to find you and say I am sorry." She seemed even more nervous and uncomfortable than I, so I got back on my bike and pedaled my way back home, never to mention to anyone my awkward offering of condolence, because, even at age 12, I was aware that most of the people I knew were not mourning the death of Dr. King, and would neither have understood nor approved of my gesture.

I imagine Marietta Green has long since joined Dr. King in the nearer presence of God. But, even so, I feel the same need all these years later that I felt all those years ago to try again, now, what I tried, then, to say: "I'm sorry." I'm sorry for Dr. King's death at the hands of an assassin all those years ago. And, all these years later, I'm sorry for the ways the popular Christianity of the Bible Belt has so often failed to embody the spirit of the One we call our Lord, especially when it comes to matters of racial justice and equality.

I know, of course, that many are inclined to dismiss a white person asking forgiveness for racial wounds and scars as "white guilt" and "political correctness." But what popular culture calls "political correctness" is more often than not the basic kindness of the Christian conscience. And what is so often derided as "white guilt" is, in fact, the moral responsibility that is inherent in having been born on the advantaged side of human difference.

In the American South, even those who, like myself, were born into families with very little money and no social standing were born, nonetheless, on the advantaged side of human difference if they were born, like myself, white, male, and straight.

Those of us who were born on the privileged side of human difference have held most of the power for most of the time, not because God wanted it that way, but because we wanted it that way. Therefore, we bear most of the responsibility for the way things have been, *and* for changing things. To live prayerfully on the path to spiritual depth is to come to see that to accept that responsibility is not white guilt or political correctness.

Words and phrases such as "white guilt," "political correctness," and "wokeness" have become the vocabulary of avoidance, the lexicon of diversion. What if all the time and energy devoted to the meaningless distraction of phrases like "white guilt," "political correctness," and "identity politics" had been given to living and speaking in thoughtful, sensitive, kind ways? For folk who look and live like myself to own our responsibility for racial injustice is not "white guilt," "political correctness," or "wokeness." Rather, it is simple, basic, no-frills Christianity:

"Do unto others as you would have them do unto you"

"Love your neighbor as you love yourself"

"Let the same mind be in you that was in Christ Jesus."

I once heard a political figure dismiss a reporter's serious question regarding white privilege with the glib colloquialism, "You certainly have been drinking the Kool-Aid." To which I thought, "Yes, indeed. We have been 'drinking the Kool-Aid' for roughly two thousand years. It is Sunday morning red. We sip it with bread. A lifetime spent drinking it has, indeed, made us mindful of the systemic inequalities that have worked for us and against others."

If we white Christians had more faithfully embodied the spirit of the One in whose name we eat the bread and drink the cup, most of the marchers in the Civil Rights Movement would have been white. Indeed, if we had more faithfully embodied the spirit of Jesus, there would not have had to be a Civil Rights Movement because we would never have stood silently by while those who were born on the minority side of human difference were marginalized and oppressed. Rather, we would have rejected our xenophobic mythology of white supremacy and the cultural hegemony it supported, not because a social movement finally forced us to, but because the Christian gospel always told us to.

There may be no more obvious commentary on how far Bible Belt Christianity is from the spirit of Jesus than the fact that the states that claim the most Christians have often been the least Christian when it comes to how those of us born on the majority side of human difference have treated those born on the other side of human difference—a sad measure of the far distance between the Jesus of popular Christianity; the I-20 Jesus, who dominates the landscape from Atlanta to Dallas; and the Jesus of Matthew, Mark, Luke, and John.

That is a history from which we should repent, about which we should make real changes, and for which we should ask forgiveness—not only from God, but also from those who have been marginalized and oppressed for no other reason than that they happen to have been born on the minority side of human difference; the small, simple, sincere act of saying, "I'm sorry"…

…sorry for our complicit silence concerning the sin of white supremacy;

…sorry for the pain so many suffered on the Edmund Pettus Bridge in Selma;

…sorry for the murderous violence that took the lives of Addie Mae Collins, Carol Denise McNair, Carole Robertson, and Cynthia Wesley on a tragic Sunday morning in Birmingham;

…sorry for the bombing of Beth Israel in Jackson; the murders of Goodman, Chaney, and Schwerner; the incarceration of the Freedom Riders; and the slaying of Emmett Till, Medgar Evers, and George Floyd;

…sorry for the countless other indignities, injustices, suspicions, and slights that persons of color have suffered and continue to endure, for no reason other than that they happen to have been born persons of color.

No, it wasn't I who committed those acts of violence and perpetuated those injustices, but it was my people. Thus, it can only be myself, and those who look like me, who say we are sorry. Those whose identity has always worked for them, not against them, are often quick to dismiss such thinking as "identity politics." But it isn't identity politics. Rather, it is basic, fundamental, entry-level "treat others as you want others to treat you" Christianity.

So, all these years later, with the uniquely heavy weight of responsibility that rests upon any person of my generation who is a white Baptist preacher in the Deep South, and with the prayerful hope that simple words can somehow travel from this side of the Jordan to the other: "Miss Marietta, I'm still sorry."

*The day we become silent about things that matter
is the day our life begins to end.*
—Martin Luther King Jr.

Todos Somos Inmigrantes

El extranjero que reside contigo será para ti como el ciudadano entre vosotros; amaréis al extranjero como a vosotros mismos.

Levitico 19:34

Esas palabras del libro de Levitico pertenecen a un grupo mas grande de versiculos en las Escrituras que recuerdan los mandamientos del Dios al pueblo de Dios con respecto a sus vecinos inmigrantes; pasajes tales como Exodo 12:49, "Habra una ley para el cuidadano y el extranjero," Exodo 22:21, "No oprimirás a un extranjero residente," Levitico 19:10, "Caundo cosechen la cosecha de su tierra, dejarán los bordes pa ra los pobres y los extranjeros," Levitico 19:33, "No privará de justicia a un extranjero residente," y Levitico 25:23, que dice que como Dios posee toda la tierra en cada país, en los ojos de Dios, todos somos inmigrantes.

No hace falta decir que, no podemos trazar una linea recta de esas palabras a nuestro mundo. Sin embargo, podemos extraer, de esas palabras, para nuestro mundo, las conclusión de que Dios tiene una prèocupación especial por las personas inmigrantes y que Dios espera que compaetamos esal preocupación.

Es posiblé que no tengamos una respuesta fácil de politica publica a los complejos problemas rela cionados con la inmigracion, sino vivir en oracion y pensatinamente en el camino hacia la profundidad nos hara saber que Dios querria que respondieramos a nuestros vecinos inmigrantes con empatia y compasión, hospitalidad, solidaria, amistad y amor.

Hace a nuestros vecinos inmigrantes sin documentos legales tieren la opcion de permanecer en su pais de origen? Si´. Pero, la mayoria de ellos toman la dificil decisión de venire los Estados Unidos debido a la desesperación y, aunque hay excepciones imegables, en mi experiencia, la mayoria de nuestros vecinos inmigrantes se encuentran entre nuestros majors vecinos. A veces eschchamos que las personas inmigrantes hacen el tipo de trabajo no todo el mundo quiere, lo que a menudo es cierto. Pero la verdad mas profunda es que personas inmigrantes no solo a menudo los trabajos no todos quieren, tambien a menudo traen un espiritu que no todos tienen; hacer que nuestras comindadades sean mas fuertes y mejores, no solo por los trabajos que realizan, pero, tambien, por la bondad que aportan.

Puedo que no lo sepamos, con certeza, lo que el gobierno deberia hacer con respecto a la inmigracien, pero si lo sabemos, con claridad, como debemos cuidar y respondes a nuestros vecinos inmigrantes; recordando que, desole Dios es dueño de todo latierra en cada nación, en los ojos de Dios todos: todos somos inmigrantes, y Dios noss llama todos a ameréis al extranjero como a vosotros mismos.

We Are All Immigrants

The alien who resides with you shall be to you as the citizen among you; you shall love the alien as yourself.

Leviticus 19:34

Those words from the book of Leviticus belong to a larger cluster of verses in scripture that recall the commandments of God to the people of God concerning their immigrant neighbors, passages such as:

- Exodus 12:49, "There shall be one law for the citizen and the alien."

- Exodus 22:21, "You shall not oppress a resident alien."

- Leviticus 19:10, "When you reap the harvest of your land, you shall leave the edges for the poor and the alien."

- Leviticus 19:33, "You shall not deprive a resident alien of justice."

- Leviticus 25:23 (my favorite one of them all), which says that, since God owns all the land in every country, in the eyes of God, we are all immigrants.

Needless to say, we cannot draw a straight line from those words to our world. However, we can draw from those words for our world the conclusion that God has a special concern for immigrant persons, and that God expects us to share that concern.

We may not have a simple public policy answer to the complex issues around immigration, but to live prayerfully and thoughtfully on the path to depth will cause us to know that God would want us to respond to our immigrant neighbors with empathy, compassion, solidarity, hospitality, friendship, and love.

Do our immigrant neighbors without legal documents have the option to stay in their country of origin? Yes. But the majority of them make the difficult choice to come to the United States out of desperation. And, while there are undeniable exceptions, in my experience the majority of our immigrant neighbors are among our best neighbors. We sometimes hear it said that immigrant persons do the kind of work not everyone wants, which is often true. But the deeper truth is that immigrant persons not only often do the jobs not everyone wants; they also often bring a spirit not everyone has, making our communities stronger and better, not only by the jobs they do, but also by the goodness they bring.

We may not know with certainty what the government should do concerning immigration, but we do know with clarity how we should care for and respond to our immigrant neighbors, remembering that, since God owns all the land in every nation, in the eyes of God we are all immigrants, and that God has called us all to love our immigrant neighbors as we love ourselves.

"*La Cancion de Bienvenida*" (The Welcome Song) is a short hymn that rises from the truth that travels in Leviticus 25:23, and that can be sung to the hymn tune GIFT OF LOVE, a traditional melody that appears in several hymnals with the hymn title "The Gift of Love."

La Cancion de Bienvenida

En los ojos del Dios,
Todas personas son inmigrantes.
En los ojos del Dios,
Nosotros todos son inmigrantes.

Todo el mundo, una familia;
Todas personas, son bienvenidas:
Bienvenido, todo el mundo,
En corazon y brazos del Dios.

Bienvenidas, todas personas.
Bienvenidos, todo aqui,
Por en los ojos, del Dios,
Nosotros todos son inmigrantes.

The Welcome Song

In the eyes of God,
All persons are immigrants.
In the eyes of God,
Immigrants all, are we.

All the world is one family,
All persons are welcome.
The whole world is welcome,
In the heart and arms of God.

All persons, welcome;
All are welcome here.
For, in the eyes of God
We are all immigrants.

—CEP

The Hour Is Coming, and Is Now Here

So he came to a Samaritan city called Sychar, near the plot of ground that Jacob had given to his son Joseph. Jacob's well was there, and Jesus, tired out by his journey, was sitting by the well. It was about noon.

A Samaritan woman came to draw water, and Jesus said to her, "Give me a drink."… The Samaritan woman said to him, "How is it that you, a Jew, ask a drink of me, a woman of Samaria?"… Jesus answered her, "If you knew the gift of God, and who it is that is saying to you, 'Give me a drink,' you would have asked him, and he would have given you living water." The woman said to him, "Sir, you have no bucket, and the well is deep. Where do you get that living water? Are you greater than our ancestor Jacob, who gave us the well, and with his sons and his flocks drank from it?" Jesus said to her, "Everyone who drinks of this water will be thirsty again, but those who drink of the water that I will give them will never be thirsty. The water that I will give will become in them a spring of water gushing up to eternal life." The woman said to him, "Sir, give me this water, so that I may never be thirsty or have to keep coming here to draw water."

Jesus said to her, "Go, call your husband, and come back." The woman answered him, "I have no husband." Jesus said to her, "You are right in saying, 'I have no husband'; for you have had five husbands, and the one you have now is not your husband. What you have said is true!" The woman said to him, "Sir, I see that you are a prophet. Our ancestors worshiped on this mountain, but you say that the place where people must worship is in Jerusalem." Jesus said to her, "Woman, believe me, the hour is coming when you will worship the Father neither on this mountain nor in Jerusalem. You worship what you do not know; we worship what we know, for salvation is from the Jews. But the hour is coming, and is now here, when the true worshipers will worship the Father in spirit and truth, for the Father seeks such as these to worship him. God is spirit, and those who worship him must worship in spirit and truth." The woman said to him, "I know that Messiah is coming"… "When he comes, he will proclaim all things to us." Jesus said to her, "I am he, the one who is speaking to you."

Just then his disciples came. They were astonished that he was speaking with a woman, but no one said, "What do you want?" or, "Why are you speaking with her?" Then the woman left her water jar and went back to the city. She said to the people, "Come and see a man who told me everything I have ever done! He cannot be the Messiah, can he?"

John 4:5-29

Those words from the gospel of John let us listen in while Jesus transcends human boundaries to embrace human differences:

…Jesus, a first-century Jew, going to Samaria, a place some first-century Jews avoided;

…Jesus, drinking after a Samaritan, a race some first-century Jews disdained;

…Jesus, talking to a woman in public, which bewildered Jesus' disciples in verse 27;

…Jesus, in John 4, saying "no" to first-century versions of twenty-first century xenophobia, racism, and misogyny;

…Jesus, transcending human boundaries to embrace human differences.

Which is the way Jesus was, which is why the deeper we go in our life with Jesus, the wider we grow in our embrace of the world. After all, there isn't another Jesus for us to get close to. The only Jesus there is for us to get close to is the one who transcends all human boundaries to embrace all human differences. So, of course, the deeper we go in our life with Jesus, the wider we grow in our love for the world. Until, eventually, we get so close to Jesus that all the human differences that won't divide in heaven don't divide on earth.

Which is not the same as saying that we do not see human differences. To the contrary, to live prayerfully on the path to depth is to see and celebrate human differences: "xenophobia," fear of the other, replaced by "xenoamora," love for the other; human difference, not erased, but embraced; all the human differences that will no longer divide in heaven, no longer dividing on earth, not because we are "color blind," but because we long for the full inclusion of the whole human family of every color and kind.

Of course, we all know that the hour is coming when, over on the Other Side, all will be welcome and celebrated. But why wait until then? Why not go ahead now and embrace the wide world in full joy? Why not let the hour of full welcome and affirmation that is coming then come now?

Which is not unlike what happened between Jesus and the woman at the well. When the woman reminded Jesus that her people, the Samaritans, had one place for and way of worship, and that Jesus' people, the Jews, had a different place for and way of worship, Jesus replied: "Believe me, the hour is coming when we will worship God neither on your mountain or mine. The hour is coming, *and is now here*, when we will worship God in spirit and in truth."

"The hour is coming, and is now here, when all these differences that matter so much to so many will no longer matter at all to any," said Jesus to the woman. Whatever those words may have meant on the ears of the woman at the well, on our ears, Jesus' declaration, "The hour is now here" means that we don't have to wait until we get to heaven to transcend all the human boundaries of our time and embrace all the human differences in our arms. "The hour is now here" means that we don't have to wait until we're over on the Other Side to move from tolerating the diversity of the whole human family to celebrating the diversity of the whole human family. In other words, "The hour is now here" means that we don't have to die before we can live.

Our business is circumference.
    —Emily Dickinson

Faith Beyond the Boundaries

After Jesus had finished all his sayings in the hearing of the people, he entered Capernaum. A centurion there had a slave whom he valued highly, and who was ill and close to death. When he heard about Jesus, he sent some Jewish elders to him, asking him to come and heal his slave. When they came to Jesus, they appealed to him earnestly, saying, "He is worthy of having you do this for him, for he loves our people, and it is he who built our synagogue for us." And Jesus went with them, but when he was not far from the house, the centurion sent friends to say to him, "Lord, do not trouble yourself, for I am not worthy to have you come under my roof; therefore I did not presume to come to you. But only speak the word, and let my servant be healed. For I also am a man set under authority, with soldiers under me; and I say to one, 'Go,' and he goes, and to another, 'Come,' and he comes, and to my slave, 'Do this,' and the slave does it." When Jesus heard this he was amazed at him, and turning to the crowd that followed him, he said, "I tell you, not even in Israel have I found such faith." When those who had been sent returned to the house, they found the slave in good health.

Luke 7:1-10

That brief gospel snapshot of Jesus' amazement at the faith of a Gentile stranger can be, for us, a small reminder that once we free God to be God beyond our religious boundaries, God will free us to see God beyond our religious boundaries.

For example, the evangelical Christian missionary E. Stanley Jones is reported to have said that, in Ghandi, a Hindu, he had found as much of the spirit of Jesus as he had ever seen in any Christian—not unlike Jesus in this gospel lesson saying that, even in his own Judaism, he had never seen such deep faith as he found in that Gentile stranger.

I had a similar experience one December day while visiting with a friend who is a Muslim. As we sat together, he said, "I know that for you, this is the season of Advent, when Christians wait for Jesus to come again. I don't know as much about Jesus as you," he continued, "But, based on what I do know about Jesus, I believe that every time anyone reaches out in love and kindness, Jesus does come again." To which I said, "Not even among Christians have I heard anyone speak in such an amazing way of the coming again of Christ."

All of which is to say that, just as Jesus in this gospel passage found faith in a person beyond the boundaries of his religious tradition, we find faith in people beyond the boundaries of ours.

Somewhere along the way, I stumbled across this powerful observation attributed to Karl Barth: "Sometimes the world humiliates the church into faithfulness." Which is, indeed, sometimes true.

A decade after the *Brown vs. Board of Education* decision, for example, the church of my childhood was still unwilling to allow people of color to worship in our sanctuary. The court in that case was closer to the spirit of Jesus than the church, the world "out-churching" the church—the way the Gentile in this gospel passage "out-Israeled" Israel.

Which, perhaps, should not be so surprising. After all, Jesus himself is reported to have said in John 3 that the Spirit of God is "like the wind," blowing where it will.

For many of us, this has been a lesson long in the learning. It has taken me a lifelong journey on the path to depth to embrace the truth that the Spirit of God is that free—as free as the wind, to stir and blow and move and go beyond the boundaries of my faith tradition. This doesn't make my faith tradition any less important to me; it just acknowledges the truth that my boundaries are not God's boundaries—

…the truth that all of our faith traditions, though they are very important and meaningful, are our interim arrangements, not God's eternal divisions;

…the truth that God is free to be with, live in, and speak through any person and every person.

In my experience, this is truth best learned not from hearing sermons or reading books, but from meeting people, actually getting to know someone who loves God from beyond our boundaries. Sometimes theology chases friendship; the wider our circle of spiritual friends grows, the deeper our grasp of spiritual truth goes.

The idea that theology sometimes chases friendship should come to us as no surprise. After all, ours is an incarnational theology. God dispatched an angel choir to Bethlehem on that night long ago to announce not the binding of a book, but the birthing of a baby…God, revealed in a Person ... and now in people—people within the boundaries of one's own faith tradition, and people beyond the boundaries of one's own faith tradition.

All of this came most fully home to me one day when I was in the presence of a person of another faith, whose life was so luminous with the love and goodness of God that, as I was walking away from our brief conversation, it occurred to me that I had experienced more of what I call "the spirit of Christ" in their presence than I sometimes find in the presence of some Christians—one of those moments in life when you find a deeper spiritual connection with a kind, gentle, loving person of another faith than you feel with some people of your own faith.

Which might, for those who grew up, as did I, with Christian "onlyism," at first be a surprise. But then you think to yourself: "Why should I be surprised to encounter the spirit of God in someone from beyond the boundaries of my faith tradition? After all, my boundaries are my boundaries, not God's. The God who created the universe thirteen billion years ago cannot be captured in anyone's religion, including my own. God is free—free to be with, live in, and speak through any person, anywhere, anytime."

The wonderful thing about learning to see, think, and live that way is this: Once we free God that way, God frees us that way. Once we free God to be God beyond our boundaries, God frees us to see God beyond our boundaries.

No one owns God.
—**Barbara Brown Taylor**

But What About John 14:6?

"Do not let your hearts be troubled. Believe in God, believe also in me. In my Father's house there are many dwelling places. If it were not so, would I have told you that I go to prepare a place for you? And if I go and prepare a place for you, I will come again and will take you to myself, so that where I am, there you may be also. And you know the way to the place where I am going." Thomas said to him, "Lord, we do not know where you are going. How can we know the way?" Jesus said to him, "I am the way, and the truth, and the life. No one comes to the Father except through me. If you know me, you will know my Father also. From now on you do know him and have seen him."

Philip said to him, "Lord, show us the Father, and we will be satisfied." Jesus said to him, "Have I been with you all this time, Philip, and you still do not know me? Who ever has seen me has seen the Father. How can you say, 'Show us the Father'? Do you not believe that I am in the Father and the Father is in me? The words that I say to you I do not speak on my own; but the Father who dwells in me does his works. Believe me that I am in the Father and the Father is in me; but if you do not, then believe me because of the works themselves. Very truly, I tell you, the one who believes in me will also do the works that I do and, in fact, will do greater works than these, because I am going to the Father. I will do whatever you ask in my name, so that the Father may be glorified in the Son. If in my name you ask me for anything, I will do it.

John 14:1-14

The thought that God cannot be captured within the confines of Christianity raises for many the question, "But what about John 14:6?—'I am the way, the truth and the life. No one comes to the Father except through me.'"

I cannot speak for you, but, as for me, my journey with those words has been a long one, a journey that began in the church of my childhood, where I learned to use John 14:6 the way everyone I knew used John 14:6, as the ultimate biblical authority for what I call "onlyism," the belief that only Christians are in the family of God in this life and only Christians will enter the presence of God in the next life.

For us, as for many Christians, then and now, few possibilities were more troubling than the thought that, ultimately, God might draw a circle of welcome around the world wider than the one we had drawn around God. So, whenever even the slightest hint of a question arose about Christianity's exclusive claim on the saving grace of God, we would shut it down by asking, "But what about John 14:6?—'I am the way, the truth and the life. No one comes to the Father except through me'"—closing down every question ever raised about onlyism.

I'm not sure why we found so troubling the idea that God's redeeming embrace might ultimately reach beyond the boundaries Christianity had established for God. I think it may, in part, have been our fear that if everyone doesn't have to believe what Christians believe about Jesus in order to go to heaven when they die, then, somehow, that might devalue the suffering of Jesus on the cross—the thought being that if God was going to redeem and reconcile all, anyway, then Jesus died for nothing. When, in fact, Colossians 1:20 says that the whole point, and ultimate effect, of Jesus' death was to reconcile the whole human family to God; the whole creation reconciled to God through what Richard Rohr calls "the universal Christ"[17]; the cosmic Christ, reconciling to God, not only all on this planet, but also the entire thirteen-billion-year-old, still-expanding, universe. Which makes the cross matter more, not less.[18]

I imagine that another part of our resistance to any consideration of the possibility that the grace of God might reach wider than the boundaries we had established around God was a more practical, institutional concern: We didn't want to lose our monopoly on the grace of God. If everyone doesn't have to believe what Christians believe about Jesus in order to enter God's family in this life, and enter God's presence in the next life, then how do we incentivize people to convert to Christianity, join the church, and give money to missionary and evangelistic organizations? All of which is a very natural and understandable human perspective, but one that sounds more like us than God, who, one imagines, does not share our institutional ambitions and anxieties.

Perhaps those were among our reasons for fearing so mightily any suggestion that the redeeming love and reconciling grace of God might be free to reach and roam beyond the boundaries of Christianity. For whatever reasons, whenever even the hint of a question arose concerning Christianity's exclusive claim on God, we would shut it down by quoting John 14:6—"I am the way, the truth and the life. No one comes to the Father except through me"—a verse that meant, in our ears and on our

The Path to Depth

lips: no one enters the family of God in this life or the presence of God in the next life except through Christianity.

Some of the best people I have ever known taught me to use John 14:6 in that way, and many sincere people of faith continue to use, and always will use, John 14:6 in that way; as the ultimate authority for Christian onlyism; the belief that if Christianity isn't the only thing, it isn't anything.

But careful speech about John 14:6 requires us to say that John 14:6, like the rest of the gospel of John, was not written to, for, or about a world religion called Christianity competing against other world religions. Rather, John 14:6, like the rest of the gospel of John, was likely written for a small, struggling, late first-century community of faith by a gospel writer who was bearing witness to Jesus as the ultimate revelation of God. Which is probably why, in John's gospel, we have that long string of verses (of which John 14:6 is one) that appear only in John; verses that seek to underscore the intimate incarnational relationship between Jesus and God, such as:

- John 8:19, "If you knew me, you would know my Father also."
- John 8:28, "I do nothing on my own, but only what the Father tells me."
- John 10:38, "I am in the Father and the Father is in me."
- John 14:6, "No one comes to the Father except through me."
- John 14:7, "If you know me you will know the Father also."
- John 14:9, "Whoever has seen me has seen the Father."
- John 14:10, "I am in the Father and the Father is in me."

Lifted out of John's gospel, and printed on a billboard or bumper-sticker, John 14:6 certainly can sound like an exclusive claim for Christianity as the only way to God. But left where we found it, in the gospel of John, it sounds like one of a long string of uniquely Johannine verses about the life of Jesus as the ultimate embodiment of the Spirit of God.

In my own long journey along the path to depth with John 14:6, I have come to believe that the ultimate Christian confession might be for us simply to say that all of God was revealed in Christ, but all of God is not contained in Christianity. As Gerard Manley Hopkins once beautifully wrote, "Christ plays in ten thousand places, lovely in limbs, and lovely in eyes, not his."[19]

To say that all of God was revealed in Christ, but all of God is not contained in Christianity, would leave us to live deeply, fully, and faithfully into our own particular Christian faith, while leaving the spirit of God free to reach and roam wherever the spirit of God will reach and roam, in this life and the next—"like the wind," as Jesus is reported once to have said.

In John 3, Jesus said that the Spirit is like the wind; blowing where it will, beyond our capacity to manage or control. And, ever since, we have been building religious fences in which to corral the wind, and raising doctrinal fortresses from which to defend the wind. All the while God, one imagines, would have preferred for us just to hang out a windchime.

*I am willing to accept that Jesus is the only way for Christians.
I am unwilling to accept that Christians get to decide
that Jesus is the only way for everyone else, too.*
—Barbara Brown Taylor

On Not Being Sad About What God Is Glad About

"Now the elder son was in the field; and when he came and approached the house, he heard music and dancing. He called one of the slaves and asked what was going on. He replied, 'Your brother has come, and your father has killed the fatted calf, because he has got him back safe and sound.' Then he became angry and refused to go in. His father came out and began to plead with him. But he answered his father, 'Listen! For all these years I have been working like a slave for you, and I have never disobeyed your command; yet you have never given me even a young goat so that I might celebrate with my friends. But when this son of yours came back, who has devoured your property with prostitutes, you killed the fatted calf for him!' Then the father said to him, 'Son, you are always with me, and all that is mine is yours. But we had to celebrate and rejoice, because this brother of yours was dead and has come to life; he was lost and has been found.'"

Luke 15:25-32

From now on, therefore, we regard no one from a human point of view; even though we once knew Christ from a human point of view, we know him no longer in that way. So if anyone is in Christ, there is a new creation: everything old has passed away; see, everything has become new! All this is from God, who reconciled us to himself through Christ, and has given us the ministry of reconciliation; that is, in Christ God was reconciling the world to himself, not counting their trespasses against them, and entrusting the message of reconciliation to us. So we are ambassadors for Christ, since God is making his appeal through us; we entreat you on behalf of Christ, be reconciled to God. For our sake he made him to be sin who knew no sin, so that in him we might become the righteousness of God.

2 Corinthians 5:16-21

"In Christ, God was reconciling the world to God's self." With those words, 2 Corinthians 5:19 takes its place alongside…

- Colossians 1:20, "Through Christ, God was pleased to reconcile, to God's self, all things, on earth and in heaven."

The Path to Depth

- Ephesians 1:9-10, "God's will, for the fullness of time, is to gather up all things in Christ, things in heaven and things on earth."
- Revelation 5:13, "Then I heard every creature, in heaven and on earth and under the earth and in the sea, singing to the one seated on the throne, and to the Lamb, blessing and honor and glory and might forever and ever"

…verses of scripture that imagine the whole human family, along with all creatures, and all creation, eventually, ultimately, eternally reconciled to God and one another;[20]

…after all the guilt has been confessed and all the responsibility has been owned;

…after all the victims have been faced, all the sin has been judged, and all the truth has been told, not without a long, hard hell of judgment, but through a long, hard hell of judgment;

…at long last, the ultimate will of God, ultimately done;

…the reconciliation of the whole world, to God;

…a possibility that is nothing but joy to many of the world's Christians, but that is as troubling to others as the father's welcome of the undeserving younger brother was to the bigger brother in the parable of the prodigal son.

Like the bigger brother in the parable, we fear that a welcome too wide makes reconciliation too easy, turning grace into a timid tolerance that allows those who do the worst to get away with the most—what Dietrich Bonhoeffer famously called "cheap grace."

And, for many, not even a long, hard hell where sin is judged, evil is purged, responsibility is owned, and victims are faced is judgment enough. The only judgment that is enough for much of popular Christianity is a hell that is endless and eternal, perhaps because so many are so uneasy with the idea of grace beyond the grave; the fear, perhaps, being that if there is the possibility of grace beyond the grave, Christianity loses the leverage to which we so often turn to incentivize people to convert to

Christianity in this life—the prospect of an eternal separation from God in the next life if they do not. And, the Bible does say that the rich man cannot escape the flames to go and be where Lazarus is, not to mention that it is appointed unto us once to die, and after that the judgment. And, those who do not believe are condemned already. And, no one comes to God except through Christ. All of that is in the Book.

But it is also in the Book that, in Christ, God was reconciling the whole creation to God's self, and that, ultimately, eternally, every creature in heaven and on earth and under the earth will sing together forever around the throne of God—the whole human family of every time and place, plus all creatures and all creation, reconciled to one another and to God. Add to that:

…Isaiah 25:6-8, which envisions a day of grace when all people will feast at the table of the Lord;

…1 Timothy 2:4, which says that God's will is for everyone to be saved;

…Titus 2:11, which says that the grace of God has appeared bringing salvation to all people;

…1 Peter 3:9, which says that God wants all to come to repentance and none to perish;

…and it causes one to wonder how universalism, the hope that all will ultimately be healed and home with God, became, for so many, heresy; while onlyism, the need for only those who believe what Christians believe to be eternally healed and home with God, became, for so many, orthodoxy.

Universalism is for some their sincerely held belief, based on some, but not all, of scripture, just as onlyism is for others their sincerely held belief, based on some, but not all, of scripture; each perspective, onlyism and universalism, with Bible to back them up, these verses versus those verses, neither perspective able to declare, with take-it-or-leave-it finality, "The Bible says it and that settles it."

Of course, even to speak of such mysteries seems, at best, awkward, and, at worst, arrogant. After all, for someone such as myself, a Christian in the Deep South, to survey the Bible to see if the Bible says that some or all will eventually be embraced in the grace of God is to speak from

The Path to Depth

a position of religious power and privilege, imposing my religion's holy book on the rest of the world—not unlike a Hindu in Calcutta or a Muslim in Tehran looking around in the Vedas or the Koran and then declaring that Christians ultimately can or cannot be embraced in the grace of God. So, whatever we say about these matters should be said, as Barbara Brown Taylor wisely counsels, with "economy, courtesy, and reverence"[21] in a voice Marilynne Robinson describes as "soft and serious" [22] and in speech that the Quakers call "gentle and plain."

To the extent that careful speech allows us to speak of such mysteries, it does seem clear that the hope, will, and plan of God is what Acts 3:21 calls "the universal restoration that God announced long ago through the prophets"; the ultimate reconciliation of the whole human family, and all creation, no matter how long it takes. That much seems clear. The great question is whether or not God will ever get what God has always wanted.[23]

Will human free will, and rejection, have the last word for all eternity? Or will God's free will, and redemption, have the last word for all eternity? Will separation and alienation have the last word? Or will God have the last word?

In words as soft and serious, and gentle and plain, as I can write or say, and with all the courtesy and reverence of which I am capable, truthful speech requires me to say that a lifetime spent on the path to a deeper life with God has helped me to come to believe that ultimately, eventually, eternally, God will get what God wants: the reconciliation of every soul God has ever loved, which is every soul who has ever lived, no matter how long it takes. Judgment, yes, because, otherwise, grace becomes a license for whoever does the worst to get away with the most. But, judgment in the service, not of eternal punishment, which God does not want for anyone, but of eventual redemption, which God does want for everyone.

…the Good Shepherd, holding out until the last lost sheep is finally healed and home;

…the ultimate will of God, ultimately done, if not on earth, at least, at last, in heaven;

…the whole world reconciled to God;

…every creature, in heaven, on earth, under the earth, and in the sea, singing together forever to the God who will not give up until every soul God ever loved and wanted is finally, fully healed and home.

Which, if it ever finally comes to pass, will, one imagines, make God as glad as the parent in the parable of the prodigal son, while also making many of the children of God as sad as the angry older brother in the story, who found in his father's boundless grace as much cause for grief as the other brother found for relief,

…a reminder for us all that one of the most simple, basic prayers we can pray is the prayer to have enough of the Spirit of God in our lives so that we will never be sad about any welcome God is glad about;

…our hope for the reconciliation of the whole creation as deep and wide as the hope and will and plan of God;

…the size of the circle of our welcome, the same as the size of the circle of the welcome of God.

*The door is always open,
Your picture's on my wall.
Everyone's a little broken,
And everyone belongs.*
—**Crowded Table**

Fields and Forests, Seas and Trees

O sing to the Lord a new song; sing to the Lord, all the earth. Sing to the Lord, bless his name; tell of his salvation from day to day. Declare his glory among the nations, his marvelous works among all the peoples. For great is the Lord, and greatly to be praised; he is to be revered above all gods. For all the gods of the peoples are idols, but the Lord made the heavens. Honor and majesty are before him; strength and beauty are in his sanctuary.

Ascribe to the Lord, O families of the peoples, ascribe to the Lord glory and strength. Ascribe to the Lord the glory due his name; bring an offering, and come into his courts. Worship the Lord in holy splendor; tremble before him, all the earth.

Say among the nations, "The Lord is king! The world is firmly established; it shall never be moved. He will judge the peoples with equity." Let the heavens be glad, and let the earth rejoice; let the sea roar, and all that fills it; let the field exult, and everything in it. Then shall all the trees of the forest sing for joy before the Lord; for he is coming, for he is coming to judge the earth. He will judge the world with righteous ness, and the peoples with his truth.

Psalm 96

"Let the heavens be glad, and the earth rejoice; let the sea roar and all that fills it; let the field exult, and everything in it. Then shall all the trees of the forest sing for joy." When those words from Psalm 96 speak of fields and forests as though they were choirs and congregations, they join a Bible-wide chorus that includes:

- Psalm 148:7, "Praise the Lord, sea monsters and fruit trees, fire and hail, snow and frost, creeping things and flying birds."

- Isaiah 55:12, where the mountains raise a concert to which the trees give a standing ovation;

- Psalm 150:6, where everything that breathes, animals and humans, praises the Lord;

- choir practice for the grand finalè in Revelation 5:13, where every creature in heaven, on earth, under the earth and in the sea—aardvarks to Anglicans, bass to Baptists, cattle to Catholics, hippos to Hindus, manatees to Methodists, seals to Sikhs, zebras to Zoroastrianists—sing glory to God together forever; all creation, fields and forests, seas and trees, singing praise to God.

All of which calls to mind, for me, that simple but powerful observation from the poet Naomi Shihab Nye: "We start with a big story, and then it shrinks."[24]

The story with which we start is as wide as the world and as big as all creation: "The trees of the forest singing for joy; the sea and all that is in it"...a story that starts out as big as all creation, before eventually shrinking to the size of the world's religions; religions that make better gates to God than fences around God, because the God who, thirteen billion years ago, created a still expanding universe, cannot be corralled inside any religion, or all religions—a 5,000-year-old Hinduism; a 4,000-year-old Judaism; a 2,000-year-old Christianity; or a 1,500-year-old Islam.

As Tennyson wrote, concerning our efforts to capture the God of fields and forests, seas and trees inside our creeds, confessions, doctrines, and religions: "Our little systems have their day, they have their day and cease to be. They are but broken lights of thee, and thou, O Lord, art more than they,"[25] ...the God of fields and forests, seas and trees, greater than all our little systems; the God of fields and forests, seas and trees, as much "out there" as "in here;" as real beyond the walls of the church as within the walls of the church.

I cannot speak of such things without thinking of Mary Oliver's testimony, "The church could not tame me, so they would not keep me... I wanted to be as close to Christ as the cross I wear; to read, and serve, and touch the linen altar cloth. Instead I went to the woods, where no tree ever turned its face away."[26]

...Oh, the boundless welcome, and judgeless embrace, of field and forest, where no tree ever turns its face away; the creation of God sometimes more true to the nature of God than the church of God.

…Little wonder that Jesus drew our attention to the birds of the air, or that St. Francis preached to a tree full of swallows in Assisi, and John Lewis to a yard full of chickens in Troy.

…And, little wonder that those who go the deepest into their own particular religion often reach the farthest beyond their own particular religion, longing for that of God which beckons beyond the boundaries that creed and confession, doctrine and religion have drawn too soon around the boundless God of fields and forests, seas and trees.

Yes is the only word a tree knows.
—Naomi Shihab Nye

Winds, woods and water
Roaring at the rim of Christendom.
—Rainer Maria Rilke

On Telling It to the Trees

Their limbs lean low
As though with snow,
'Neath the weight of all
The news they know.

Their trunks so full,
When felled and milled,
The pages emerge
Already filled;

With heart-rending longings
And knee-bending words,
Which only the years
Of the trees have heard.
—CEP

The Journey Jonah Never Took

When God saw what they did, how they turned from their evil ways, God changed his mind about the calamity that he had said he would bring upon them; and he did not do it. But this was very displeasing to Jonah, and he became angry. He prayed to the Lord and said, "O Lord! Is not this what I said while I was still in my own country? That is why I fled to Tarshish at the beginning; for I knew that you are a gracious God and merciful, slow to anger, and abounding in steadfast love, and ready to relent from punishing. And now, O Lord, please take my life from me, for it is better for me to die than to live." And the Lord said, "Is it right for you to be angry?" Then Jonah went out of the city and sat down east of the city, and made a booth for himself there. He sat under it in the shade, waiting to see what would become of the city.

The Lord God appointed a bush, and made it come up over Jonah, to give shade over his head, to save him from his discomfort; so Jonah was very happy about the bush. But when dawn came up the next day, God appointed a worm that attacked the bush, so that it withered. When the sun rose, God prepared a sultry east wind, and the sun beat down on the head of Jo nah so that he was faint and asked that he might die. He said, "It is better for me to die than to live."

But God said to Jonah, "Is it right for you to be angry about the bush?" And he said, "Yes, angry enough to die." Then the Lord said, "You are concerned about the bush, for which you did not labor and which you did not grow; it came into being in a night and perished in a night. And should I not be concerned about Nineveh, that great city, in which there are more than a hundred and twenty thousand persons who do not know their right hand from their left, and also many animals?"

Jonah 3:10-4:11

"When God saw that the people of Nineveh turned from their evil ways, God changed God's mind concerning the calamity God had said God would bring upon them, and God did not do it. This was very displeasing to Jonah, and he became angry." With those words, the book of Jonah reminds us that, though Jonah traveled many miles in the small book that bears his name, there is one journey Jonah never took. Jonah fled to Tarshish at the beginning of the book of Jonah, sailed to Nineveh near the end, and, between those two journeys, traveled to the bottom of the sea in the belly of a fish. But those many trips taken and miles amassed notwithstanding, there was, apparently, one journey Jonah never took: never going far enough with God to get close enough to God to rejoice over God's wide welcome and boundless grace.

In fact, God's grace for the Ninevites made Jonah so angry that Jonah said he would rather die than watch God be that good to the Ninevites—Jonah, mad about the same wide welcome God is glad about.

I often wonder where that comes from, the need for some to be excluded from the welcome of God in order for us to be happy with our inclusion in the welcome of God.

I was once that way, like Jonah, grumbling at the thought of too much grace for too many others. The grace God gave to others did not take an ounce of grace from me, but, even so, I would have rather God be left with leftover love than for anyone to have it who didn't get it the way I got it.

But, then, somewhere along the way, I moved beyond that. I cannot say exactly when it happened, but I do have an idea how it happened. I believe it was the daily practice of praying to get on and stay on the path to a deeper life with God.

This long, slow journey is open to all of us: staying on the path to depth so carefully and prayerfully for so long that, eventually, we reach the wide and wonderful place at which the size of the circle of our joyful welcome becomes the same as the size of the circle of God's joyful welcome; a long, slow journey Jonah may never have taken, but one that any of us can begin any time we choose.

*I live my life in widening circles that reach out across the world.
I may not finish the last one, but I give myself to it.*
—Rainer Maria Rilke

Epilogue

The path to depth is a long and narrow way which, traveled prayerfully enough for long enough, will, eventually, bring us to the wide and wonderful place in life at which we are never sad about any inclusion God is glad about, and never glad about any exclusion God is sad about.

Notes

[1] Mary Oliver, *Thirst* (Boston: Beacon Press, 2006) 69.

[2] Thomas G. Long, *What Shall We Say?* (Grand Rapids: Wm. B. Eerdmans Publishing Co., 2011) 115.

[3] Mary Oliver, *Devotions* (New York: Penguin Press, 2017) 337.

[4] Elizabeth Gilbert, *Eat, Pray, Love* (New York: Penguin Press, 2006) 358.

[5] Mary Oliver, *Thirst* (Boston: Beacon Press, 2006) 69.

[6] ForbesLife, Mar. 12, 2007.

[7] Naomi Shihab Nye, *Words Under the Words* (Portland, OR: Far Corner Books, 1995) 42.

[8] Barbara Brown Taylor, *An Altar in the World* (New York: HarperCollins Publishers, 2009) 170.

[9] As quoted in Ann Lamott, *Traveling Mercies* (New York: Pantheon Press, 1999) 102.

[10] Mary Oliver, *Thirst* (Boston: Beacon Press, 2006) 58.

[11] Ernest Hemingway, *A Farewell to Arms* (New York: Charles Scribner's Sons, 1929) 249.

[12] W.H. Auden, *The Age of Anxiety* (Princeton, NJ: Princeton University Press, 2011) 105.

[13] Peter Storey, *With God in the Crucible* (Nashville: Abingdon Press, 2002) 67.

[14] Mary Oliver, *Devotions* (New York: Penguin Press, 2017) 55.

[15] Remember, the word "homosexuality" did not exist until the nineteenth century. Thus, it does not appear anywhere in scripture.

[16] For helpful articles on these passages, see *The New Interpreters Bible*, vol. 10, Leander E. Keck, ed. (Nashville: Abingdon Press, 2015), 858-859 and *Mercer Dictionary of the Bible*, ed. Watson E. Mills, Roger Aubrey Bullard, Edgar V. McKnight (Macon, GA: Mercer University Press, 1990), 386-387.

[17] Richard Rohr, *The Universal Christ* (New York: Convergent Books, 2019).

[18] This, of course, assumes that God was alienated from humanity and needed reconciling to humanity. This assumption is at the center of the idea that Christianity is primarily about a problem (alienation) and how to fix it (reconciliation). The question is whether or not that is true. Is God as prone to alienation as humans? Does God need reconciliation the way we do? Is Christianity primarily about a problem and how to fix it, or is Christianity primarily about a life and how to live it and a love and how to give it?

[19] Gerard Manley Hopkins, *Poems and Prose* (New York: Alfred A. Knopf, 1995) 18.

[20] This assumes that God was alienated from humanity and needed reconciliation to humanity. Is that true, or is alienation a human problem that we have projected onto God? Is the language of alienation and condemnation that we use to describe God's posture toward humanity something that God says about people or something people say about God?

[21] Barbara Brown Taylor, *When God Is Silent* (Lanham, MD: Cowley Publications, 1998) 117.

[22] Marilynne Robinson, *Gilead* (New York: Picador, 2004) 55.

[23] William Willimon, *Who Will Be Saved?* (Nashville: Abingdon Press, 2008) 46.

[24] Naomi Shihab Nye, *Words Under the Words* (Portland, OR: Far Corner Books, 1995) 132.

[25] Alfred Lord Tennyson, *Selected Poems*, Aidan Day, ed. (New York: Penguin Books, 1991) 130.

[26] Mary Oliver, *Thirst* (Boston: Beacon Press, 2006) 29-33.

CPSIA information can be obtained
at www.ICGtesting.com
Printed in the USA
LVHW080907021222
734417LV00004B/496